THE
FLEECING
OF
AMERICA

THE
FLEECING
OF
AMERICA

☆ ☆ ☆ ☆ ☆

Senator William Proxmire

BOSTON
HOUGHTON MIFFLIN COMPANY
1980

Library of Congress Cataloging in Publication Data
Proxmire, William.
The fleecing of America.
Includes index.
1. Grants-in-aid—United States. 2. Government spending policy—United States. I. Title.
HJ275.P76   336.3'9'0973   79–28550
ISBN 0–395–29133–X

Printed in the United States of America

v 10 9 8 7 6 5 4 3 2 1

A portion of this book has appeared in the *New York Times Magazine.*

To the long-suffering American taxpayer

Contents

THE
FLEECING
OF
AMERICA

(1)

The Fleecing of America

THIS BOOK tells the story of the Golden Fleece of the Month, an institution I established some five years ago to expose the most outrageous example of federal waste in the preceding month. It provides numerous examples of spectacular taxpayer rip-offs on ridiculous spending programs. It also analyzes the immense pressure on the Congress to spend the taxpayers' money and suggests a program that can stop it.

After years of complaining about the outrageous waste of federal money and the explosion of spending that has characterized our government's policy over the last decade, I decided to establish a monthly award for the most absurd example of waste accomplished by one federal agency or another during the preceding thirty days.

We thought of several titles: Rip-Off of the Month, Spending Crime of the Month, Give-Away, Throw-Away, and so forth. We finally settled on *fleece* as the proper word for a smooth, legalized theft from the taxpayers, and Tom van der Voort, our appropriations expert on the staff, and a Greek mythology buff, proposed to call it the *Golden Fleece Award*. *Golden* because this was real money, not play money, but coin of the realm—out of the taxpayers' pockets—and *Golden Fleece* because the Greek myth has application.

Jason sailed forth with fifty helpers in the good ship Argo to capture the Golden Fleece. But it wasn't the pushover for Jason that it is for modern fleecers. Among other obstacles, his Golden Fleece was guarded day and night by a never-sleeping dragon. The United States taxpayers have no such dragon guarding their gold, or, if there is one, he must have been sound asleep for some time. The mission of this book is to awaken the guards and sentinels of our federal resources and give to all of you who contribute to them an understanding of the dangerous ease with which they are being dissipated.

The amounts actually spent on many of the federal agency grants singled out for Golden Fleece awards is very small compared to overall federal extravagance. The military, public works, cities, corporations going broke, and many other petitioners at the public fountain take up more millions of our half-trillion dollar budget than research projects, as we shall discover during the course of this book. But, like every vote, every dollar counts.

Why do so many of our officials decide to spend the taxpayers' money in ways that are patently futile and for no general good? One reason is that with a budget of such mammoth size—far beyond the ability of most of us to envision—there is no way that the President, his cabinet, or members of Congress, no matter how diligent or dedicated, can do more than set up the broadest kind of spending guidelines. Immense discretion, often lacking in officials of greatly varying ability and vulnerability, must be relied on. Many officials, when faced with a request for a research grant, fail to ask themselves the simple question, "Who really cares what the answer to this investigation is?" Sometimes the answer obviously is, "No one."

Another reason is the attitude that the country is so vast, so rich, so limitless in its resources that a few thousand federal dollars spent here and there don't matter. This is what Senator Ribicoff means when he talks about the "play money," or "fountain pen money," approach that is at the root of so much impulse spending.

Then there is the inevitable factor of plain greed. This is of course not confined to researchers; it exists to some extent among countless petitioners—all the way from the highest to the lowest echelons. But it was a researcher who pointed it up in an ill-timed book (he was on the verge of getting a grant from the National Institute of Mental Health [NIMH]) called *Academic Gamesmanship.* It is strange how he could have been so tactlessly overcome with his own wit to write the chapter on grants in which he notes (p. 104) that "not all disciplines are in an equally good position to milk the government and the foundations."

On page 108 he explains that "in drafting a research proposal, the primary concern should be to write it in such a way as to appear worthwhile to the evaluators rather than to give a candid description of what you intend or hope to accomplish; hence the need for dishonesty."

His tongue-in-cheek humor verges on dismaying reality when he writes:

> In addition to paying part of your basic salary, grants will typically also give you an extra two months of summer salary. You can finance numerous jaunts to domestic and international conferences out of your research money without having to beg your university for it or having to justify your trip by reading a paper. And, if your research calls for going overseas, you can lead the life of an oriental potentate with an American income in a low cost-of-living country. Should you remain an expatriate for eighteen months or more, you even get a $20,000-a-year tax exemption for waving the star-spangled banner from the halls of Montezuma to the shores of Tripoli (p. 107).

A few pages later he advises that a good budget must "show two qualities: it must be both detailed and extravagant."

This researcher practiced what he preached, and it is to the credit of the scientific panel which reviewed his original application that they considered his budget highly inflated, and to the credit of NIMH that they gave him somewhat less than he requested. It is not to their credit, however, that they failed to estimate what, if any, value this research had for the American taxpayer. Furthermore—and this is par for the course with NIMH—they failed to press the researcher or his associate for the required final report and copies of all published works which flowed from this particular grant.

It was a grant of $97,000 to study ethnic and class relationships among Indians and non-Indians in several communities in the Peruvian Andes. After my staff insisted that NIMH obtain the final report, which was already three years overdue, an article entitled "The Peruvian Brothel, A Sexual Dispensary and Social Arena" was finally turned in. In it the researchers (the article was not written by Dr. Van den Berghe, who obtained the grant originally) explained how a one-year investigation of the brothel was conducted. "Twenty-one prostitutes were formally interviewed and many more were interviewed informally. In addition, the staff of the brothel was interviewed, especially the madam. . . . By visiting the brothel at various times, it was possible to get a good idea of its everyday functioning." A good amount of detail follows.

Of course, the researchers were occupied by other things than brothels during their eighteen-month stay in Peru. Several articles and two books on various subjects were produced, such as:

- Ethnicity and Social Structure in the Inca Empire
- The Use of Ethnic Terms in the Peruvian Social Science Literature
- Aymara-Quechua Relations in Puno
- Inequality in the Peruvian Andes, Class and Ethnicity in Cuzco

It is sad and ironic to report that NIMH knew nothing about the one-year brothel research until a member of my staff questioned them about it. Nor did they contact the researcher and ask him for his overdue report until my staff insisted. Dr. Van den Berghe did finally send a very short final report but refused to supply NIMH with copies of the books produced with the help of federal dollars. In an imperious moment he told a NIMH official that all his books were available for purchase. How do you like that? After a $97,000 fleece!

I certainly do not object to academic researchers studying either brothels or ancient Inca vestiges. What I protest is the federal government paying for it. With the need for mental health research here at home so great, and research budgets so tight, it is unbelievable that NIMH gave this project funding.

Other examples of projects receiving Golden Fleece awards should suffice to prove the failure of some agency officials to use discretion, not to mention common sense.

*

Would pregnant pigs be less bored if they jogged? The Department of Agriculture wanted to answer the question: If you put a gestating pig on a treadmill, would you reduce her psychological stress in confinement?

As an avid jogger myself, I think we need more joggers in this country, but spending money to psychoanalyze hogs at the taxpayers' expense seems to me going too far.

One of the ironies here is that though raising pigs in confinement has some recognized advantages—more economical use of land, mechanized feeding, getting the animals fatter faster, and possibly cutting down on disease—it is not clear whether there is anything to be gained by keeping sows in confinement when they are pregnant. We do know that neither the litter nor the weight per baby pig is increased. And once the USDA researchers began to study these cooped-up pregnant sows, all kinds of problems surfaced, including lack of exercise, which led to world-weariness and tension. Therefore, federal funds were and still are being spent on devising a treadmill to make them happier.

The confinement method is, according to the USDA, used in from 40 to 50 percent of this nation's hog production, and it may well be the wave of the future; but we may need an exercise treadmill for mother pigs during gestation. All such intervention will leave us in the world of George Orwell, linking his two masterpieces, *Animal Farm* and *1984*. But at the moment it seems ridiculous to put pregnant pigs in confinement and spend federal money to ease their boredom.

I am not saying this research should not be done; perhaps some good will come of it. But in this case the question that every agency official should ask himself—Who really cares?—is crucial, because if there is any prospect that a new technique of caring for sows in gestation will be productive, the vigorous and wealthy meatpacking business with its direct, explicit interest in the subject will spend the funds to develop it. Why should the taxpayer subsidize it?

*

The pig-jog grant did not get our first Golden Fleece Award. That went, after some indecision, to the National Science Foundation (NSF) for spending $84,000 on a study of why people fall in love.

Our indecision was caused by having to choose between so many other idiotic studies of almost no significance to anyone.

Consider our choices. We found that the NSF was going to spend $181,000 to study the social behavior of the Alaskan brown bear; another $121,000 to examine the African climate during the last Ice Age; and $25,000 for a study of primate teeth, this one from the Internal Revenue Service (IRS). That one, of course, has scientific value as part of the body of anthropological knowledge, and I can see approval of a Ph.D. thesis in this area. But not $25,000 ripped out of the federal budget!

Yet I felt that our very first Golden Fleece Award had to be for the $84,000 to find out why, how, and for how long men and women are attracted to each other. I objected to this fiscal fling not only because no one—not even the NSF—can argue that romantic love lies in the realm of science, but also because I believe firmly that even if they spent $84 million, or even $84 billion, they wouldn't come up with anything the great majority of Americans would profit from. Or believe. Or even want to hear about. Some things in life should remain unprobed by science's scalpel, and right at the top of the list of those things is the mysterious phenomenon of romantic passion. The National Science Foundation should stay out of this field where they don't belong and leave it to poets and mystics, to Irving Berlin, to thousands of high school and college bull sessions, Dear Abby, Ann Landers, not to speak of Havelock Ellis and Alex Comfort, and a cast of hundreds of others.

Do we really want some official message on falling in love? Is there anything about spending federal money that will rationalize it to anyone's satisfaction? Of course not.

This first Fleece Award brought on a certain amount of rebuttal flack which I will describe in another chapter. It came primarily from faculty at the University of Wisconsin (the NSF gave them $260,000 and Harvard $121,600 for similar studies) in defense of their University of Minnesota colleague, Professor Elaine Walster, a social psychologist. For my part, I do not care whether the project is done at Harvard or at Minnesota or in my home state. If it's a waste of the taxpayers' money, it should not come out of the federal budget.

*

Why do rats, monkeys, and humans clench their teeth? Did that question ever bother you? Bother you enough to feel that our government should spend $500,000 to find some kind of answer? As a matter of fact, the Office of Naval Research, the National Science Foundation, and the National Aeronautics and Space Administration spent that much and more to get the answer.

A lot of interesting things turned up.

Anger, giving up smoking, and loud noises produce jaw clenching.

People get angry when they feel cheated and not only clench their jaws, but tend to scream and kick.

Monkeys get mad when they are given an electric shock. They try to avoid that shock.

Drunken monkeys don't usually react as quickly or as often as sober monkeys. Hungry monkeys get furious more quickly than well-fed monkeys.

It seemed obvious to me that it was time for the federal government to get out of the monkey business and we gave those agencies a Golden Fleece; some humans got very angry and the legal proceedings went all the way to the Supreme Court. But that's a story I want to tell you a little later on.

*

Why are people rude and why do they cheat and lie on tennis courts? If you play tennis, I'm sure this question has bothered you plenty, especially if you use local public courts and find that someone else has taken the court you reserved in advance. But would one ever imagine that the federal government would make a federal case out of it and hand over $2500, all the taxes paid a year by a typical American family, to experts in sociology and ethics to investigate such behavior?

It happened indeed, and I gave a Golden Fleece, thereby calling a double fault on the National Endowment for the Humanities for its grant to Arlington County, Virginia, to study why people are unruly and ill-mannered and why they lie about the time they started to play and resist requests to prove local residency. It was claimed by the funders and fundees that it was important to find out why tennis players get frustrated and mad when they have to wait for hours or go from court to court to find a place to play.

As for the manners of tennis competition, one has only to watch Ilie Nastase or Bob Hewitt throw tantrums on television to get the idea that tennis is no more a love game than football. Or read about the increase in crime throughout the country to guess why there now is more vandalism than there was earlier of tennis nets, cables, cranks, and lights.

Yet a $2500 grant, matched by in-kind services of the county, was given in order to

1. hire the consulting services of a professor of sociology;
2. hire the consulting services of a professor of ethics and philosophy;
3. conduct a survey of the attitudes of about 300 players toward the local tennis regulations, and evaluate results;
4. conduct two public meetings during which, among other experiments, the professors guide the local tennis players in role-playing activities in which they take the part of the suffering local tennis buffs.

Studying why human beings are competitive is hardly my idea of a national spending priority.

*

How long does it take to cook breakfast? For some reason, the U.S. Department of Agriculture (USDA) crashed through with a Golden Fleece winner by spending $46,000 on the cooking of eggs for breakfast. One might infer a vague connection with the chicken industry, but that would be a false scent. It seems the money really went to help McDonald's, Burger King, and IHOP with their employee schedules and labor costs. Which answers the fundamental question, "Who cares?" Not the run-of-the-mill taxpayer who is footing the bill.

The study came up with the world-shaking discovery that it takes 838 "measurement units" to fry two eggs in a skillet. In case you are wondering, a time measurement unit, or TMU, is something that was also cooked up by the merry spenders at the USDA. They decided to declare a TMU equal to 0.036, that is, thirty-six one-thousandths of one second.

It would take less time to fry six eggs and eat them than to translate those TMUs into seconds on your handy calculator. However, thanks to the $46,000 study, when some guy asks you how many homers Gil Hodges hit for the Brooklyn Dodgers in

1950, you can come right back with your question: How many TMUs does it take to cook a six-ounce order of hash? The answer: 1222.

You don't have to wait that long for a nice breakfast. You know from the study that you can get some french toast in only 960 TMUs.

But I'm not being fair; you get more than that for your tax money. Refinements abound. In the case of french toast, for example, the USDA tells us that it takes 22 TMUs to get the egg and only 15 TMUs to break that same egg against the bowl. And so it goes.

In all seriousness, why should you and I pay for information that may or may not be useful to McDonald's and Roy Rogers? If anyone at the USDA had paid the slightest attention to the way the food service industry operates, with their time and motion studies, their training schools, their meticulous analysis of new technology to be sure it will pay for itself before they spend a nickel to introduce it—if the USDA had made the most casual kind of inquiry, they surely wouldn't (or would they?) have allowed the $46,000 rip-off.

*

What do you do with a completely useless dictionary? If you think this question too harsh, consider this gouge out of the national budget accomplished by the Smithsonian. They spent nearly $89,000 to have a dictionary produced in Tzotzil. What is Tzotzil? It's an obscure and unwritten Mayan language, spoken by 120,000 corn-farming peasants in southern Mexico who also speak Spanish.

Even more fascinating and esoteric, this particular dictionary records only the specific dialect of Tzotzil spoken by only about 10,000 members—a mere one-twelfth—of this Mexican group of Mayan descendants.

There are no Spanish definitions in the dictionary and thus, as the author of the dictionary himself admits in his introduction, the volume is essentially useless, even in southern Mexico.

But let's give the Smithsonian their day in court. What do they say in their defense?

In *their* preface to the dictionary, they declare:

> General dictionaries of obscure languages are not fashionable, but if the understanding of human cultural behavior is the goal of anthropology, and if language is, in a sense, "a mirror for man," the pragmatic and semantic investigation of man's socially patterned linguistic habits is surely relevant.

I know a few people, and so do you, who would buy that. But the author's estimate of the dictionary is a little harder to take:

> I have been asked how I secured the information in this dictionary. And aside from the techniques described for the botanical section, I have no answer. I know that sober or drunk we laughed and groaned and chattered in the "true language" for ten days and ten years, in museums, and on mountain trails, shivering in icy San Cristobal rooms, and basking beneath a Zincantec sun.

So the $89,000 was not completely wasted. Somebody had some fun, though nobody may ever use the dictionary as it was intended. For, as the author says frankly and colorfully:

> My main regret is that this dictionary bears heavy witness to the school of imperialistic anthropology—lacking Spanish definitions, it could have but one use for the Zincantecs, the same alluded to discreetly by Don Juan, "You know what we do with paper in Mexico."

As senator from the state that produces more toilet tissue than any other, I don't think the Smithsonian should compete with one of Wisconsin's major industries.

Finally, referring to his tome, the recipient of the $89,000 grant predicts it will soon "collect dust on library shelves."

I recognize that some of these statements, including the last, were made tongue-in-cheek. I appreciate the candor and humor. But this doesn't help in justifying the taxpayer funds spent on such a project. Here's a fleece that tells us loudly and clearly that we need a set of priorities that our bureaucracy will respect and stand by firmly.

*

What does burning paper in the sky look like? The National Endowment for the Arts made a $6025 grant to an artist to film the throwing of crepe paper and burning gases out of high-flying airplanes.

They made this grant—to be sure a small bit of the $123.5 million of federal money they will spend this year—in order to "document on film an event designed to alter an audience's immediate environment for a short period of time," according to Ms. Nancy Hanks, the endowment's chairperson.

One hopes there was a fair crowd of taxpayers there to have their immediate environment altered as four one-mile-long crepe-paper rolls were thrown out of two small planes over El Paso, Texas, helped along by two sky divers who reeled them out and accompanied them to the ground.

Another group of citizens, in Pennsylvania, was treated to the sight of a team of skydivers parachuting down to earth, wearing backpacks of glowing gases.

According to Ms. Hanks's letter to me, funding for this project was based on the review of past work of the artist by a panel of experts. The artist's earlier work, not paid for by the federal government, had included crepe-paper drops in three states as well as drops of bouquets of plastic streamers, tire rubber, and even thirty-five rolls of toilet paper. The artist told my staff that the latter made lovely patterns as it dropped from the sky but that crepe paper is even better. She explained that her work calls attention to the higher spirit of mankind and the coming era of peace and harmony on earth.

Some of the $6025 went this way: $1424.28 for airfare and lodging for the artist and her husband, who served as cameraman, for a week's stay in February on the Caribbean island of

St. Martin. It was necessary, we were told, to visit this resort island in order to film one of the environments which had influenced the development of the artist. She also explained that she needed the unique combination of beach, sky, flowers, and wall paintings found in that part of the world for her movie.

Then there was $1713.32 for airfare, meals, car rental, and airport parking for the artist, her husband, a sky diver, and two of the artist's children, who were the ground crew assigned to retrieve the crepe paper.

The movie, which runs about twenty minutes, was sent to the National Endowment for the Arts only after my staff asked to see it. This film (the artist retains the copyright) contains only brief glimpses of the crepe-paper and lighted-gas drops. Much of it consists of various scenes of the artist posing in St. Martin. She says it has been well received by her peers.

Lots of fun and fascinating for the artist and her family. But for the 200 million other Americans who theoretically benefit from federal spending, this remains just another yawn-producing home movie.

While I strongly support the idea of free expression of all creative artists, and believe that the crepe-paper-dropping artist sincerely believes in the importance of her work, I see no reason for the federal government to pay for this kind of frou-frou.

*

Who really pays for such fun and games? The worker who trudges through the factory gate at seven every morning to spend a grueling day on the assembly line pays. So does the cleaning woman who spends all night—five nights a week, year in, year out—scouring floors in a Madison Avenue office building. The dairy farmer in Marathon County, Wisconsin, who rises at 5:30 A.M. to milk his cows and puts in a day of work that lasts until he harvests his hay crop by the dim light of his tractor long after sunset, also pays for this artistic fling.

While the $6025 grant is relatively small, it is the sum total of the taxes paid by the three typical American citizens I have just listed.

What these seven Golden Fleeces demonstrate is the casual, even arrogant disregard, on the part of some officials, of where the money they are dispensing comes from. Each case may represent a small fraction of the federal budget. But the fruits of the attitude that federal money somehow doesn't count, multiplied to the millionth every year, is at the heart of much of our waste.

These foolish expenditures also point up the failure of many an official donor to ask and insist on a convincing answer to the simple question, Who cares?

The fact is that a group of people get pleasant, sometimes even thrilling, assignments without providing anything that a reasonable number of citizens would dream of paying for if the IRS didn't extract the funds from them on pain of imprisonment, and then turn them over to grantsmanship experts to have a ball.

Take these two more examples of fun at our expense:

The Federal Aviation Administration (FAA) spent $57,800 on a head-to-foot physical study of 432 airline stewardesses, involving 79 specific measurements.

A well-turned ankle or calf may help in getting a job with the airlines. Yet the study showed that the young women calipered before acceptance at the American Airlines Stewardess Training Academy in Fort Worth may be unique. Why? Because, as the study says, "Although all airlines recruit stewardesses from the same general population of young females, each has its own selection standards for age, height, weight, education, and other variables." Which means, of course, that the anthropometric figures gathered from the bodies of stewardesses training in Texas have almost no general relevance. And whether in inches or centimeters, this FAA anthropometrical project doesn't measure up to the $57,800 it cost. It's just plain waste.

The study has other fatal flaws in addition to being unrepresentative of North American stewardesses in general. Aircraft designers, for whom the research was presumably done, learn that weight varies from 94 to 145 pounds; height from 5 feet 1 inch to 6 feet 1 inch; busts from 24 to 37.5 inches; and waists from 21 to 28. About all that can be said to designers of safety equipment is that stewardesses are young women with the body measurements of young women.

Second, information of equal value was available from anthropometric data already gathered on WAF recruits, student nurses, and college women. The minimum-maximum requirements of the airlines concerning height, weight, age, hip girth, and so forth, were also well known.

Third, there's a peculiar irrelevance in some of the 79 measurements, to wit:

- skin fold of the upper arm and posterior calf
- vertical height of the sphyrion
- popliteal length of the buttocks
- the transverse distance between the centers of the anterior superior iliac psines
- the knee-to-knee breadth while sitting
- maximum horizontal width of the jaw across the gonial angles
- the height of the nose.

Most important, why should the government pay for this study at all? It is proper for the FAA to set standards and require airlines and aircraft manufacturers to meet them. But the cost of screening stewardesses to fit their airplanes should be borne by the private profit-making companies. There might then be a greater incentive to do needed research studies rather than this one, which duplicates previous findings and, what is more, is based upon a useless sample.

There was another fun-and-games grant that deserves brief mention. The National Science Foundation spent 46,100 tax dollars to find out if environmental distractions such as sex, humor, and empathy would reduce the honking of frustrated drivers during city traffic jams.

Bikini-clad maidens were tested out first. In this "sexual

arousal" aspect of his experiment, Dr. Baron had his traffic-jumping female "dressed in an extremely brief and revealing outfit of a very unusual type." Perhaps the Women's Movement should take notice. The humor and empathy experiments also used females—one strolled around in an "outlandish humorous clown mask," and the other "hobbled along on crutches and wore a bandage on her left leg."

Everything worked. The young male drivers smiled at the near-naked one and watched her walk down the street, and some whistled or made the expected comments. But the other two research accomplices also stopped the honking.

Evidently there must have been some money left to burn, so Dr. Baron went on to discover that people who literally get hot under the collar when caught in a very warm room become aggressive unless cooled off by a drink of iced lemonade.

It would be fortunate if tensions and aggressions of city drivers could be reduced. But are the NSF officials who authorized the $46,100 trying to tell us that all we can do about it is to organize thousands of young women wearing bikinis or clown masks, or carrying crutches, to strut, dance, or stagger across every busy intersection in every big city in every rush hour?

Aside from the sexual discrimination involved, that's a rather drastic way to reduce unemployment.

(2)

Fleeces of Many Colors

BY THE END of the last chapter we began to move into the wasteland of useless projects. There are some others that may have seemed at first glance to ask purposeful questions but which at second glance would have inspired any responsible official to ask, "Don't we already know the answer?"

It is hard to believe, and appalling, that $38,174 was spent by the Environmental Protection Agency (EPA) to find out (surprise!) that the run-off from open stacks of cow manure on Vermont farms was causing the pollution of the water in nearby streams and ponds. This research is an example of solid waste in spending. There's not a dairy farmer in all of Wisconsin or Vermont who didn't know the answer already.

The University of Vermont Animal Sciences Research Center contributed $29,040 to the project and conducted the study on a Vermont dairy farm. Thus the total figure was $67,214. The only vaguely sensible aspect of the study was a questionnaire answered by 874 dairymen about what they might do "both in the presence and absence of external regulation."

Here are the major conclusions as quoted in the final report:

> The concentrations and amounts of nutrients in run-off from the manure storage facility were high enough to cause deterioration of water quality in small streams and ponds.
> The run-off from such a facility should be confined in a lagoon and

irrigated on cropland, *or* the manure stack should be covered to eliminate the large volume of contaminated run-off.

Covering for the facility should probably be a permanent roof rather than a thin plastic sheet placed directly on the pile. The latter is cumbersome and not very efficient.

Coming from the number-one dairy state, I strongly favor economic studies with a sensible cost/benefit ratio in support of milk, dairy farmers, or the cow. This study could have been slanted not at a question any farmer could answer but at finding inexpensive ways to prevent the run-off from manure. When my staff pointed this out, the EPA projects officer agreed, even though the study did not go in that direction.

The EPA was taken for a ride by the canny Vermonters—and so were the American taxpayers.

Here is an even more rampant example of asking questions that any fool could answer—this one to the tune of $222,000. The Federal Highway Administration (FHA) authorized research to ask drivers in three states how they felt about the big, fat trucks that swarm over our highways. They concentrated on nine sites: rest stops, parking garages, turnpike exits, and so forth, and here are some of the questions they asked:

Do you consider that large trucks

a) contribute to traffic congestion?
b) block a driver's vision?
c) travel too fast on highways?
d) travel too slow going up hills?
e) make a side splash on wet roads that is a problem?
f) make smoke and fumes that might be a problem?

I'll donate my own car to the FHA for experimental purposes if the answer to these questions is not a resounding *yes.* In fact, when interviewed motorists find out how much is being spent on the survey, they will get even madder than they do at the big trucks.

This study cannot be justified on grounds of safety or how drivers actually *behave* when confronted by big trucks. Instead, it centers on their attitudes. Most galling, it is merely a $222,000 blow-by-blow description of a $1 million study called "The Effect of Truck Size and Weight on Accident Experience and Traffic Operations," and another one, costing $297,633, on "The Effects of Truck Size on Driver Behavior."

In spite of the obvious redundancy, this study of "motorists' attitudes toward large trucks" is justified by its sponsors on the following grounds:

> In examining questions of commercial vehicle/passenger car interactions, the research focus has been on the aerodynamic and human factors aspects. The thrust of these studies was on the physics of interaction and the psychophysical performance of drivers. Rarely were questions relating to *social* perception, cognition or affect ever addressed. The cognitive or mentally evaluative dimension of such vehicular interactions or potential interactions was lost in error variance or not considered at all in formulations of aerodynamic disturbance functions and driver performance factors.

So much for previous studies and possible duplication. And so much, too, for the English language.

The original prospectus was also shrouded in the jargon of the social sciences. American drivers and all other donors to the national budget will be glad to know that the researcher "will be expected to develop a multidimensional attitude measurement device" in order to "collect sufficient behavioral data to relate each attitude dimension to its associated behavioral correlates," and to "define in detail the experimental design, including statistical analysis paradigms."

Just a small amount of one-dimensional attitudinal common sense would have saved over $60,000 for some more vital cause —such as reducing taxes.

*

What'll it be like in 2025, Daddy? This is not a question with an obvious answer, but one that cannot possibly be answered.

The Department of Transportation (DOT) spent $225,000 on

a report that forecasts transportation needs in the year 2025. They whomped up four separate science fiction "scenarios" in which the United States is transformed by (1) an Ice Age; (2) a dictatorship; (3) a hippy culture; and (4) a society that has blossomed into what the authors term the American Dream.

This may be the most impractical study ever paid for by the government.

What do we get for our money? We get a few of the usual truisms, such as, if there were an ice age by 2025, "a very large number of people will be forced or attracted to move to the South and Southwest to escape an undesirable climate." We are also warned that if there happened to be urban guerilla warfare at the beginning of the twenty-first century, "cities would need more transit police, automobile use in afflicted regions would become risky, and damage insurance rates would rise astronomically."

The predictions get quite specific: in an ice age society hitchhikers will be "ubiquitous, even riding on roofracks" and drivers who pick them up will "charge about 25¢ for local trips." As for the cost of gasoline: in the ice age, it will be $1.70 per gallon, only $1.50 in a hippy society, but $1.80 under a dictatorship. In the American Dream scenario gas goes down to $1.05. We are not told what sorts of fuel discoveries, conservation, or development of solar energy go into this estimate.

But we are told that if there is an ice age by 2025, "it will no longer be socially unacceptable to attend a business meeting or social engagement in traditional walking, bicycle, or motorcycle attire."

In the first, chilling scenario, "Anne Jamison awoke with a start, shivering involuntarily. She'd been dreaming of endless expanses of swirling snow beneath a slate grey sky."

In the second, where a way of life rules that is called "voluntary simplicity" and which values frugality and harmony with nature and inner spiritual development, we have a slightly familiar character description:

Jud wanted a rug that was predominantly light blue, and he had been collecting old jeans for months. They would take all the buttons and zippers off to save before the weavers ripped the old clothing into strips . . . In his introspection he had found the courage to adopt a new way of living that was more rich and rewarding than anything he could have imagined. And he had the courage to accept himself, warts and all, for the person he was and wanted to be. Yes, personal growth was difficult but very satisfying.

In a third imaginary future, America comes out of a depression as a "disciplined society" where a "bureaucratized leadership, faceless and diffuse, would have at its disposal sophisticated psychotechnology." Railroads, as in Mussolini's Italy, would "run efficiently . . . and on time."

In the traditional American Dream future, Americans who have continued "to move toward rising affluence" have made the "post-industrial society" a reality by 2025. It is a world of high technology, sophisticated communication, and high levels of consumption.

Statistics flesh out these imaginary futures. For example, interest rates, which neither the Office of Management and Budget nor the Council of Economic Advisors can predict even a year in advance, will be 4 percent in a year-2025 hippy society but 12 percent in an ice age.

What does the $225,000 report recommend that the DOT do in the face of these alternative futures?

The authors urge their readers to study a new rail cargo transport system and then "solve the legal, organizational, financial, union, and political problems attendant in bringing such a special intermodal rail network into existence."

They also throw in a recommendation that we develop improved sailing ships for a possible ice age, dictatorship, or hippy society. We should also develop nuclear-powered ships for a possible "success" future.

Perhaps the Department of Transportation should consider abolishing their futuristic research division, and devote themselves and the federal moneys they obtain to present needs rather than to nightmares and dreams.

One of the most preposterous examples of fleecing originated, ironically enough, with the Law Enforcement Assistance Administration (LEAA), which spent nearly $27,000 to determine why prisoners want to escape from jail.

This is beating a dead horse with a vengeance. Is there any possible reason for such a study? Or anything more obvious than its conclusion that "escape is both a function of the characteristics of individuals and the situations in which they find themselves"?

The findings rest heavily on the responses of the inmates themselves to a questionnaire. Can anyone be sure that they would give straight answers to the researchers?

Furthermore, the conclusions are couched in such technical and obscure language as to reduce to a great extent any usefulness they might have in helping predict which prisoners are most likely and which prisoners least likely to escape. This evidently was the motivation of the study. Such knowledge might reduce the costs of recovering escapees and of providing more security than is necessary.

Which sounds great. I am all for these goals of escape prediction and cost reduction. But how many prison officials will be equipped to translate the following:

> The increase in predictability of escape from R-.64 when secondary variables are used singly and R-.61 when questionnaire variables are used singly to R-.77 when both are used conjointly, empirically demonstrates that escape is associated with both static and dynamic factors.

It is easier (far too easy, in fact) to follow their conclusion that the escaper is more likely than other inmates to be one who has been "turned down for parole" or "not scheduled for parole review." But is it so surprising to hear this fact?

In a second conclusion the study reported that, "Analyses

tend to depict the escaper, particularly the multiple escaper, as a career criminal." Is anyone dumbfounded by this finding?

A third profound "implication" of the study is that there are certain "critical times" for escape, such as "when an inmate is first admitted or transferred to a unit, when his program progress is stalemated, when he encounters family difficulties, and when he feels his security threatened."

The man on the street knows as much. Yet that same American average citizen was forced to foot the bill for these truisms.

Let me be very clear. I am not saying this study is all bad. Its objectives are good, and some of its contents may be helpful. But we must have a set of priorities when it comes to spending and the deficiencies of this study make it, in my view, not worth the money spent.

A few years ago I was one of two U.S. senators to vote against reauthorizing the LEAA. We wanted to abolish the agency entirely. Had we been successful, this $27,000 would not have been wasted.

*

Another category of foolish waste involves expenditures that simply have no purpose—research money poured out to find (or not find) a conclusion that can have no possible bearing on general human well-being or on behavior. These are projects that no sane person, no business, and no local or even state government would dream of financing.

*

Are sunfish that drink tequila more aggressive than sunfish that drink gin? This was one part of an experiment on fish that researchers, sponsored by the National Institute on Alcohol Abuse and Alcoholism (NIAAA), performed while observing what it means to be "stewed to the gills."

The fish section of the experiment cost the government $102,000; at the same time the NIAAA funded another study, to

the tune of $90,000, which boiled down more or less to trans-
forming rats into alcoholics by making them neurotic. They were
placed in frustrating situations and given unpredictable rewards
and shocks.

As a matter of fact, the NIAAA has spent literally millions of
dollars on hundreds of experiments to turn normal rats into
lushes with little or no success. The justification is that rats share
some biological features with human beings, and their alcoholic
behavior might shed some light on human drinking habits. Are
young rats more likely than adult rats to booze in order to reduce
anxiety? Can rats be systematically turned into permanent alcoholics? Many university animal experimental laboratories
have been kept busy and well funded in pursuing this foolish
goal.

For while it is clear that the testing of mice has been invaluable
in cancer and other physiological research, both rats and fish are
so much lower on the evolutionary scale than man that experiments on their psyches can tell us very little about complex
human problems involving nerves, emotions, lifestyles, and, if
you will, the spirit.

The NIAAA has the important responsibility of combating
the most extensive and tragic drug problem that has ever faced
our nation. They say they need additional funds. Then why waste
their allotments on watching sunfish let loose their aggressions
when they are stoned?

*

Should your tax money be spent to teach college students how
to watch television? The Office of Education (formerly part of
HEW) spent $219,592 to develop a "curriculum package" which
will, according to the funding contract, enable college students
to "distinguish between television's fact and fiction, recognize its
various viewpoints, and evaluate its messages." For example,
they investigated "how weekly viewing of 'Rhoda' affects the
viewer's attitude toward divorce or more broadly toward femi-
nism."

If students' TV viewing sophistication has not been developed by college age, one seriously doubts whether this expensive curriculum package can help them. They may anticipate an easy *A* in the course called "TV Viewing 101"; but the Office of Education deserves a solid *F* for this contract.

Under its Special Projects Act, the Office of Education has in fact developed some outstanding television programs, such as "Sesame Street" and "The Electric Company." It has also funded four contracts totaling $823,651 to develop "critical television skills" at the elementary, middle, secondary, and post-secondary school levels, and another $800,000—to train teachers and distribute the materials developed and tested in phase one —is contemplated.

Considering the amount of violence on TV plus the attempts of advertisers to aim their shots at children, there is some justification for the elementary, middle, and secondary school level proposals. But spending $219,000 for the college program is absurd and should be canceled.

It is to be undertaken by the School of Public Communication at Boston University and it proposes to "help viewers to understand the differences and the values of various types of television programming, i.e., commercials, drama, soap opera, situation comedies, documentaries, public affairs, news, sport programs."

At the ages of eighteen to twenty-four or older, viewers will "become aware of the differences between an issue presented in a television drama (fiction) and the same issue treated in a television documentary (fact)."

Phew!

In our culture young men and women may not know how to spell by the age of twenty-one, but there's one thing they do know backward and forward, and that's TV—in all its vagaries and hoaxes.

The next thing will be federal funding to develop "critical skills" in college with which to watch football, shop for Christmas gifts, or shovel snow.

The study proposal is replete with modern testing jargon. You

have your "target populations," "impact evaluations," "delivera-
bles" under the contract, and so forth. Here is a good chewy
paragraph.

> A series of univariate and multivariate analyses will be performed
> in order to delineate the characteristics of the sample in terms of
> pre-test level of critical viewing skills, as well as sociodemographic
> and other variables, and the effect of the test curriculum. Among
> these analyses will be a multiple analysis of variance . . . In addi-
> tion, multiple regression analysis and canonical correlation will be
> used to assess the relationships between the critical viewing skills
> on one hand, and on the other, sociodemographic and other varia-
> bles.

Is it possible that those who wrote that paragraph could write
a textbook to provide "an understanding of the relation between
television programming and the printed word"?

The grant raises a series of issues. If needed at all, why
shouldn't such a study be done by individual university faculties
to fit their own specific curricula, and the materials be developed
and produced by one of the many textbook publishing houses?
Should the federal government be offering inducements for the
proliferation of new courses to take up the limited time students
have for fundamental subjects?

In my view, in this period of inflation and budget stringency,
or in any other period, the money should not be spent at all.
There is ample literature in the field already. Why couldn't college students develop their TV and other media savvy by reading
Newton Minow, Vance Packard, or Marshall McLuhan rather
than taking courses provided by $219,000 of federal money, and
based on univariate and multivariate analyses delineating the
sociodemographic, dependent, and independent variables, all
nicely assessed through multiple regressions and canonical corre-
lations?

*

The same study that's been done sixty-seven times before is now under way, to the tune of $245,000. It's a study of New Towns, which, over the last decade, have been studied to death as most of them lay dead or dying. We need a new study as much as Boston needs cod or Jimmy Carter needs peanuts.

The new Department of Housing and Urban Development (HUD) new-town study, entitled "Analysis of Administrative Problems in the Title VII New Communities Program," is being done by Booz-Allen. Its real purpose is to determine why new towns have gone broke. However, that question has been answered time and again. New towns require such a massive investment before there is any cash flow that neither private enterprise nor government subsidies can make them profitable. Just ask anybody who has tried to sell their bonds.

The Library of Congress has furnished me with an annotated bibliography which lists sixty-seven new-town studies. The funding of new towns, the government of new towns, new towns in town, the supporting system of new towns, the sociology of new towns, and on and on. You name it, they've studied it.

Some of these studies were government funded, some privately funded, and some jointly funded. HUD itself has funded at least a dozen, at a cost of more than $1.5 million in the last few years. And in 1973–1974 the National Science Foundation spent $1.2 million for a major new-town study conducted by the University of North Carolina which in my view was a shockingly unnecessary duplication.

New towns have been studied by the Urban Institute, the Council of State Governments, the Environmental Protection Agency, HEW, the Alcohol, Drug Abuse, and Mental Health Administration, the Ford Foundation, the Rockefeller Brothers Fund, the Cleveland Foundation, the Conference of Mayors, the Douglas Commission, and dozens of others.

The sad fact is that most government-financed and many privately financed new towns have gone bust. HUD is sponsoring no new ones now and, in the parlance of the trade, both public and private developers "broke their picks" on new towns.

Before an agency funds a study it should at least take the trouble to find out what has been done in the past. Apart from the Library of Congress listings, there is unfortunately no central place where descriptions of existing or previous studies are available. The right hand of the government does not know, and more often than not does not even try to find out, what the left hand of the government has studied or is proposing to study.

Obviously a *sixty-eighth* study of a failed experiment in community planning simply has no real purpose. The $245,000 was wasted as surely as if it had been put into twenty-dollar bills and burned in your fireplace.

*

I am all for technological inventions—but have you heard about the back-wheel-steering motorcycle no one, but no one, can ride? The National Highway Traffic Safety Administration spent $120,126 on one that their own tests, completed *before* the granting of the contract, showed it would be difficult if not impossible to steer. This is the ultimate example of the taxpayer being taken for a ride.

In September 1977, in spite of repeated warnings by experts, the agency issued the contract to a California firm to design and test a motorcycle with a low center of gravity powered by the front wheel and steered by the back wheel. Some agency officials thought this low-slung configuration would make the motorcycle safer. There was something magical in the backward angle that the highway men couldn't resist. It turned out that it would take either a Superman or a Wonder Woman to manage it.

As the contractor dutifully sought to improve the design of the bike, every computer simulation showed it was harder to control than the toughest bucking bronco. On January 9, 1978, the contractor reported "the lack of controllability of the rear-steered configuration, indicated by computer results so far," but persistent officials told him to try again.

On February 3, both the contractor and the subcontractor were ready to give up and asked to be allowed to stop work, but again agency officials insisted that the backward project go forward and demanded that the bike be built and tested.

By April the contraption was completed and the contractor confirmed what the National Highway Traffic Safety Administration had known all along: the rear-wheel-steering motorcycle was completely unridable, whether going forward, backward, or sideways. In fact, the builders had to add training wheels to prevent serious injury to their testing victims. Sometimes expert cyclists could not keep the motorcycle upright for even one instant. The longest ride, which was 2.5 seconds, appeared to involve a lucky twist of the wheel at the right time.

By this time the agency officials finally admitted that back steering was a flop, but the bureaucratic urge to compound errors made them decide to continue experiments—this time on a front-steering, low-slung model—despite more warnings from experts. While the contractor pointed out the problem of controlling the cycle at rest and the reduction of rider and passenger comfort, the editors of *Cycle Magazine* warned of more dangerous problems.

[The contractor] is currently working on a Honda with a seat height comparable to that of an average car—about sixteen to twenty inches. That puts the motorcyclist's head right at headlight level and removes from him one of his great advantages: his ability to see over the tops of cars, and to be seen by the occasional driver.

So here was the perfect machine for a government man. It didn't work forward, it didn't work backward, and whichever way it went, if you were driving it, you couldn't see very far.

The climax of federally funded technological tomfoolery came with the donation of a cool $2 million for the completely unworkable police car. This is the story of a patrol car that ended up as a highway-bound spaceship on wheels. Such an experimental car would make James Bond green with envy and should leave any taxpayer purple with rage.

Fortunately, because its load of problems exceeded even its load of gadgets, plans for field testing the model car were halted. But not until $2 million had been drained from the federal treasury to pay for this monstrous experiment.

What we have here is an idea that might originally have had some merit. But the car was so trucked out with one gold-plated item after another that it ultimately became the heaviest Golden Fleece of them all.

What was the purpose of the Law Enforcement Assistance Administration's "Police Patrol Car System Improvement Program"? According to the agency, the objective was to incorporate into this jewel "the expressed requirements of the police community for a number of technical improvements and the evaluation of an improved police car to enhance capabilities, utility, safety, economy, and, ultimately, police officer productivity."

As far as police officer productivity is concerned, the officer who was thrust behind the wheel of this wonder car would have a lot on his mind besides crime prevention. In addition to normal driving concerns, he would have to worry about his multiple spark discharge ignition system while grasping in his hand his voice/digital terminal while reading his heads-up display while listening to his audio recorder while looking at his wide-angle periscope rearview mirror.

Maybe with a little practice he could manage that much. But he would also have to keep tabs on his carbon monoxide monitor, use his voice/digital transceivers, operate his microcomputer mass memory, at the same time keeping a watchful eye on his digital cassette reader and his keyboard.

Furthermore, in spare moments, if he has any, he must check his tire sensor, his brake-wear sensor, his catalytic convertor/exhaust temperature sensor, and seven different condition sensors.

This car, a good example of "too much and too soon," might

be custom-produced for an oriental potentate with a chauffeur fresh out of MIT, but it's hardly a model to be mass-produced for average working patrolmen.

And anyone who believes that a car with all these guzzling gadgets·would get more miles per gallon and have lower maintenance costs might just as well believe that the tooth fairy is alive and well in Keokuk.

The LEAA itself has realized some of the shortcomings of its prototype: The multiple spark discharge ignition system "was prone to failure while the vehicle was in operation" and "did not demonstrate any substantive improvement in vehicle operating economics."

As for the hands-free voice communication systems, the agency's report says: "Where officers must hook their radios as well as themselves into the system, rapid ingress and egress, especially under stressful situations, could be hampered by the additional necessary disconnect/connect functions." Translation: They could get stuck in the car.

As for the hand-held audio/digital terminal, it was on the big side, since it included the terminal, batteries, and the two way radio. The battery's life, by the way "was quite short due to the high power requirements of the display."

It was also doubted whether the wide-angle rearview mirror could meet all specifications "without expensive roof modifications."

Other difficulties contributed to the demise of this project after two million tax dollars had gone down the drain.

An outside nonofficial analyst provided further reasons why this project was a ridiculous waste of federal funds. Two points in particular stood out.

First, the median price, in 1976, of the LEAA police car package would have been $49,078 per automobile, above and beyond the sticker price of the car itself. It was assumed that a city or county would initially invest in twenty prototype cars, choosing "sophisticated features" midway between the lowest and highest priced. Where in the world would local governments get that kind of money, even if the cars were worth every penny?

Second, this analyst had discovered that the opinions of working police were ignored by the LEAA in developing this jewel— a charge supported in a General Accounting Office report on the agency. Clearly this omission on the part of the LEAA is indefensible, especially when we stop to realize that the kind and amount of equipment in a police patrol car may mean the difference between life and death for the driver.

*

Do we really need it right now? and Could we do it for less money? are two other questions that agency officials seem loath to answer.

The Space Program has been an exciting and proud success for our country and deserves our praise and gratitude for a job well done. But even the space program doesn't justify luxurious and wholly unnecessary waste; such as millions for moon rocks.

The National Aeronautics and Space Administration (NASA) has requested $2.8 million to construct an addition to the existing Lunar Receiving Laboratory at the Johnson Space Center to house 100 pounds of moon rocks. The fiscal irony of NASA's request is that it is not needed. In 1971, after spending $9.7 million to house the moon rocks, NASA curator Dr. Michael Duke indicated that the building would be "the permanent facility for storage, handling and doing detailed studies of the rocks."

It is appalling to think that taxpayers who shelled out nearly $15 billion for the Lunar Exploration Program are now being asked to pay $2.8 million to construct an addition to a perfectly adequate $9.7 million concrete structure. For, in spite of Dr. Duke's statement, NASA is back on Congress's doorstep for more housing for the rocks. What makes their request all the more shocking is that, since 1965, the space agency has paid out $10,786,676 in research and development expenditures for lunar sample examination and study. They are stocked with expensive storage and research equipment, plus a Remote Storage Facility at Brooks Air Force Base in San Antonio, Texas, where they are keeping a representative portion of the lunar collection. The public must surely be asking, "How much is enough?"

NASA argues that the new addition to the laboratory is needed "to insure that the lunar samples are adequately protected against natural and man-made hazards for the foreseeable future." This statement closely follows their assessment that "the present Curatorial Facility has operated successfully since 1971 to support an active lunar sample research program that involves several hundred scientists mostly from American universities." And it still remains unclear what "hazards" NASA has in mind. The present building is a massive structure and most observers admit that almost nothing short of a bomb blast or gigantic earthquake could penetrate the whole maze of concrete buildings that make up the mammoth Johnson Space Center in Houston.

If the space agency is so concerned about natural or man-made hazards, they might consider using several empty Titan silos— lying dormant in the hills of Montana—which the Air Force has been trying to unload for years. These silos can withstand the force of an atomic bomb.

Placing footprints on the moon was one of man's greatest achievements, and the moon rocks are an important American treasure. But NASA has a perfectly adequate facility in which to house and study them. Twenty million dollars has already been spent on the rocks; an addition to the space complex at Houston would be a wasteful indulgence.

Though the space agency should indeed engage in activities where the payoff may be remote, some of their proposals in this era of inflation should be challenged and, in my judgment, defeated. Take, for example, their pressure to pluck from the federal budget millions to find intelligent life in outer space.

The wave of popular enthusiasm for close encounters of the third kind does not seem to justify NASA's proposal to spend from $14 to $15 million over the next seven years to conduct, in

Pasadena, California's Jet Propulsion Lab, "an all sky, all frequency search for radio signals from intelligent extraterrestrial life."

But this is only the foot in the door. Under the heading of "broad objectives" NASA indicates that the purpose of the study is to "build an observational and technological framework on which future, more sensitive SETI (Search for Extra-Terrestrial Intelligence) can be based."

What's wrong with this program? Like so many other big spenders, this is a low-priority program which, at this time, constitutes a luxury the country can ill afford.

The study is predicated on the assumption (which of course is theoretically possible) that extraterrestrial beings are out there beyond our solar system trying to communicate with scientists here on earth. If NASA has its way, untold millions will be spent on this theoretical possibility at a time when people on our earth —Arabs and Israelis, Greeks and Turks, the United States and the Soviet Union, to name a few—are having great difficulty communicating with each other, sometimes over a span of a few miles.

Furthermore, NASA could have selected a much less expensive way to intercept messages probably sent 10 to 15 billion years ago on our time scale. A much more economical, more narrowly focused SETI proposal from the Ames Research Center (costing $6.5 million over seven years) was rejected in favor of the $14 to $15 million Jet Propulsion Lab project. And to add insult to injury, NASA has told my staff that what they might do is plug in the Ames project so that both would be operating at the same time.

As (one hopes) the "last of the big spenders," NASA spent $140,000 for a 6000-word article and a follow-up book-length history of the Viking-Mars project. This was presented on a silver platter to a young man whose major claim to authorship fame is an unpublished history of the Apollo-Soyuz space venture, written for NASA, plus a series of articles on small arms that appeared in such publications as *Gun Week* and *Rifle Magazine.*

For his initial 6000-word article, he will receive $20,000 plus $4,000 in expenses. This means $4 a word. After he delivers a written report regarding available historical documentation, NASA will exercise the option clause of the contract, which means $116,000, including $6160 in expenses, for a book-length manuscript of between 100,000 and 150,000 words.

Perhaps the most eminent official federal history was Samuel Eliot Morison's *History of the United States Naval Operations in World War II.* This work of massive scholarship appeared in fourteen volumes between 1947 and 1960. The late Commander Morison was easily the equal of Barbara Tuchman or John Toland. How much did the navy pay for these remarkable volumes? Not $130,000, or even $30,000, but $15,000 for each long volume, and I understand the navy received more of a return in royalties than was spent on producing the books, which attests to their value and popularity.

To put it another way, the author NASA chose for the Viking-Mars project is receiving more for his 6000-word article than Commander Morison got for writing an entire volume. In fact, if the commander had received the $4 a word the NASA writer is getting, he would have been paid $300,000 or $400,000 per book. Even allowing for inflation, this price discrepancy is fabulous.

Why did NASA accept the young author's proposal without bothering to see if there were other qualified authors who would do the job for less? Apparently the prime reason was that this author got his foot in the door with a $73,850 contract to immortalize the joint U.S.-USSR space docking venture. Although this manuscript has not been published, the author demonstrated an "ability to work smoothly with NASA managers and technicians . . . doing this in such a way as to avoid irritating the sources of information." One can only deduce that the author is writing a sanitized government history of the Apollo-Soyuz operation without asking embarrassing questions.

(The taxpayer should know that NASA has spent $1,378,391 since fiscal 1969 on the research and writing of "official histories." A history of the Saturn program will cost $307,742 more, while it will take $174,628 to commemorate Skylab and $60,500 for an administrative history of NASA.)

One cannot blame the author who has received the Viking-Mars publishing plum. But NASA should not be spending these vast amounts to establish its own image. The publishing marketplace can supply the need, if such a need exists. And in this particular case, they should have gone through the normal procedure of investigating current established historians, as well as seeking the recommendations of the NASA Historical Committee to select potential authors, rather than let the contract on a sole-source basis to a writer whose qualifications consist largely of magazine articles plus a still unpublished book commissioned by NASA itself.

The Golden Fleece awards have served a purpose in alerting the public and Congress to many instances of outrageous waste. But they are only the tip of the iceberg, which is almost entirely submerged and invisible and far, far bigger than most people imagine.

(3)

Opponents of the Fleece
and Some Offshoots

I THINK the Golden Fleece awards have been a useful way to remind both the bureaucracy and the public, as well as the Congress, how extravagant our government has become. There have been some good results. Many of the programs cited, and others which will come up later in this book, have been reduced or eliminated entirely.

But does the good outweigh the bad? Some think the Fleece awards should be stopped. They describe them as mean, cruel, petty, an appeal to the know-nothing, anti-intellectual bumpkins of our society. They accuse them of being anti-research, calling them attempts to belittle, with obvious attempts at humor and sexual come-ons, the uphill efforts of the scientific and academic community to push back the frontiers of knowledge.

I am attacking, they say, the sponsoring of the sort of genius that carried Columbus to the discovery of a new continent, Thomas Edison into the harnessing of electricity, and stirred Einstein to produce a quantum jump in man's understanding of the universe. In an article in the *New York Times* on April 1, 1979, Dr. Robert Jastrow, director of NASA's Goddard Institute for Space Studies, approvingly quoted Dr. Bruce Murray's contention: "If astronomers at the beginning of the 20th century had listened to arguments like Senator Proxmire's, the most important discoveries—pulsars, quasars and radio astronomy—would never have happened."

This opposition to the Fleece is imposing and certain of its grounds. Take, for instance, the legal challenge.

On April 16, 1976, Dr. Ronald Hutchinson, a Michigan scientist who had earned his doctoral degree in experimental psychology at Yale, brought suit against me for a sum that eventually reached $8 million.

He sued me for giving a Golden Fleece Award of the Month to three agencies for funding his research into why monkeys, rats, and humans clench their jaws, at a cost to taxpayers of $500,000.

By 1979 the case had reached the Supreme Court.

Dr. Hutchinson charged that Morton Schwartz, who had done the research, and I had "libeled, slandered and defamed" him, and that my statements had "held him up to public ridicule and damaged his professional reputation."

The Hutchinson summons further charged that he had "suffered injury to his feelings, had been humiliated, held up to public scorn, suffered extreme mental anguish and physical illness and pain to his person." Furthermore, he had allegedly "suffered a loss of income and ability to earn income in the future," since, as the result of the Golden Fleece Award, he was unable to acquire new research grants, funds, and employment contracts.

The Hutchinson suit obviously has a point and raises a question that deserves an answer. This country has benefited immensely from federally supported scientific research. Government agencies should not be bullied by United States senators or by anyone else into fearing or hesitating to award funds to serious, competent scientists to do research that may benefit Americans. And certainly this country would lose out if scientists were so intimidated by fear of ridicule that they became unwilling to apply for government funds.

This danger could be particularly acute in the many areas of scientific inquiry that may be of great value but superficially appear to be silly.

Any criticism of scientific research spending should be informed, careful, and sensitive to this danger.

In the case of the jaw-clenching fleece, the staff man who did the work on the award, Morton Schwartz, is a former professor of economics at Lawrence University in Appleton, Wisconsin. Along with his background in economics he had some training in psychology. He first heard of the funding for the study from the editor of a science publication. After ascertaining what agencies were funding the study—NASA, the Office of Naval Research, and the National Science Foundation (NSF), with some help from the state of Michigan's Department of Health—he called on each of them and secured the documents that rationalized the funding. He also spent many hours conferring with the officials responsible for the Hutchinson grants.

He then conferred with Howard Shuman, my administrative assistant—a former economics professor at the University of Illinois—and me. We discussed the jaw-clenching study in detail, considered what justification there was for spending the $500,000 of government money, and concluded it was a waste of public funds, worthy of the Golden Fleece.

I then told Schwartz to prepare a release announcing the award to the three federal agencies involved and explained our reasons. Shuman read and edited the release; I made a few changes and additions. We decided before publishing it that Schwartz should call Dr. Hutchinson and get his reaction.

Schwartz phoned Dr. Hutchinson, read him the text of the release, and advised him that it had been prepared on the factual basis of his own materials and reports.

Dr. Hutchinson told Schwartz that the release did not evaluate his work fairly, and said that he would make his own statement in rebuttal. He did so, and ultimately carried his plaint into the courts.

While Dr. Hutchinson took exception to my conclusions

throughout the case, there has never been a challenge to any fact contained in my original speech. Furthermore, the courts found that even if I were not immune from a suit, and even if Dr. Hutchinson were not a "public figure," a position the Supreme Court agreed with, there was no defamation or libel in any of the jurisdictions where libel might be said to have occurred.

People say, "You'll be careful in the future!" The answer is we were careful and responsible. The district court found no libel, but I was sued for $8 million nonetheless.

The basic issue the Hutchinson case raises is whether a citizen has a right to criticize to the point of ridicule what he regards as a waste of the money he pays out in taxes. In this case, the issue was especially sharp. Here's why: I happen to serve as chairman of a Senate appropriations subcommittee that has jurisdiction over a series of appropriations, including those allocated to NASA and NSF—two of the three agencies that funded Dr. Hutchinson's research. As chairman of that subcommittee I had more than a right, I had a clear duty to examine, discuss, and call to the attention of my colleagues and the public as a whole every aspect of the spending under our jurisdiction as vigorously and forcefully as I could, and to use humor and any other rhetorical device I felt necessary to point up a fiscal abuse.

Dr. Hutchinson and those who agree with him, including the agency officials who sponsored him, have every right to respond in kind, and just as vigorously.

Some argue that this is unfair because a U.S. senator has a big advantage in his ability to command media attention. But I can assure you that an offended researcher or agency official has no trouble persuading the press to carry his response. Reporters recognize the importance of balance and I can't recall a single instance during the awarding of more than fifty Fleeces when reporters failed to try very hard to secure rebuttals from all concerned.

What's wrong with this kind of debate? If I am wrong in my

criticism, the public can decide after hearing both sides.

One of the most fascinating reactions to criticism of wasteful spending of the taxpayers' money on research has come from the university community. As one of the most articulate groups in America, they should be the most eager to enter the lists of free and full debate over the merits of a research grant involving the public's, not private, money. Yet their response has not on the whole been enlightened with any details of counterargument that would convince the general public that their tax money went to a generally useful cause or convince me and my staff that we made a blunder.

Here's how it went. As I have said, our first Golden Fleece Award went to an $84,000 grant from the National Science Foundation to a University of Minnesota social psychologist to study the causes of romantic love. Then, on March 18, 1975, I issued a public statement criticizing a similar but more expensive grant to the University of Wisconsin to study passionate love.

A summary of this project, obtained from the NSF, states:

> Social psychologists have generally tried to explain passionate love within the reinforcement paradigm. Since data have not fit tidily into this framework, the investigator will turn to Schachter's theory to explain strong interpersonal attraction.

In language equally cryptic, at least to all but psychologists, the NSF report further tells us that the research will rely primarily on "the implications of Schachter's general theory of emotion, which suggests that the emotion an individual will experience depends on how he labels his feelings."

The researchers focused on three questions:

1. How can arousal be best defined?
2. Can the form of physiological arousal really generate all or almost all emotions—given appropriate labeling?
3. Can individuals relabel their feelings and under what conditions is this likely to occur?

One of the investigating methods used to measure "arousal" was to give participating students at the university caffeine tablets and then arrange a "simulated date" in the laboratory for these students with members of the opposite sex.

This sort of study may have some value for psychology scholars and even a small number of therapists, but to soak the taxpayer for more than a quarter of a million dollars for it is a disgrace. The National Science Foundation failed at that point to recognize that the federal budget is limited and that there is an unlimited variety of problems we could explore with federal money. This means that the NSF should operate under a system of rigorous priorities. I think it's time to put a stop to their federal version of "the love machine."

Passionate love and sexual arousal, to be sure, are fascinating subjects. But thousands of people have been writing about, talking about, and researching this favorite subject for centuries. The recent flood of books, movies, and TV expositions is overwhelming. Free enterprise and the profit motive do not and never will by-pass the rich payoff in the field of sex. Commercial and academic publishing houses are the natural outlets for both the superficial and the distinguished scholarly efforts to pigeonhole how we feel and how we "label" what we are feeling when we are doing "what comes naturally." The NSF grant constitutes an appalling disregard of any reasonable system of priorities.

What was the answer my criticism triggered from the university people?

Their rebuttal referred only to the grant of $84,000 given to Professor Elaine Walster at the University of Minnesota and made no reference to the $260,000 distributed to researchers at the University of Wisconsin. They did not deign to justify either research project, their position being more or less that attacks should not be made on academics who get grants but on the donors who give them. The University of Wisconsin's Faculty Senate passed the following resolution at its meeting on April 14, 1975:

The UW-Madison Faculty Senate deplores the damage that is being done to basic research and to freedom of scientific inquiry by irresponsible and inaccurate attacks of the kind Senator William Proxmire recently made on research supported by the National Science Foundation including research conducted by one of our colleagues, Professor Elaine Walster.

We fully endorse a legitimate concern for economy and for watchfulness in Federal Government support of scientific research, as in every other realm of government activity. But we must respectfully point out that Professor Walster's study had undergone rigorous review through every appropriate scientific and administrative channel. Her own recognition as a Fellow of the American Psychological Association and of the Society for the Psychological Study of Social Issues are further evidence of her scientific integrity and productivity.

Subsequent events have made it clear that Senator Proxmire did not fully understand nor try to find out the true nature of the project. Professor Walster's research on equity relationships between employers and employees, donors and recipients, engaged couples, husbands and wives, and parents and children is mocked by the Senator's characterization of this work as a study of "passionate love" addressed to "erotic curiosity." It is significant that the Senator released his condemnatory statement after he had asked Professor Walster for further written information but before there was time for him to receive her reply.

Decisions regarding the value of basic research must continue to be based on peer reviews. To the extent that in his personal opinion some funded basic research projects are wasteful, Senator Proxmire's criticisms must be directed at improving the Foundation's policies and review criteria. To instead make attacks on individual scientists' projects, through the mass media and on insufficient knowledge, is a threat to freedom of scientific inquiry which the Faculty Senate can only view with deep dismay.

Here again, I grant the opponents of the Golden Fleece awards a good point. Indeed, a senator involved with appropriations should work with a foundation such as the NSF to improve their overall methods of selecting research for funding, including the "peer review" system. I have worked with the National Science Foundation to precisely this end, and we have achieved some improvements in procedures.

1. In response to my so-called irresponsible attacks, the NSF has established an awards accountability branch which will be responsible for enforcing grantees to comply with the requirements for reports before closing out its awards.

(In the case of the Peruvian brothel researchers' fleece of the National Institute of Mental Health, the agency never received any final reports or reprints of articles and books. NIMH personnel have told my staff they are also trying to improve their post-award control.)

2. In light of the Fleece award to the NSF involving conflict of interest in a consumer credit study, the agency has updated and classified employee conflict-of-interest and standards-of-conduct regulations.

3. In order to prevent future confusion about other and previous funding of work, the NSF has developed a standardized history of principal researchers, proposals, and awards made.

4. In response to my direct request, the NSF now publishes a brief description of completed awards each year.

5. An Office of Audit and Oversight was established in 1977. In addition to improving general audit functions, this office now makes a full review of 6 percent of all awards to see if procedures are being followed during the life of the award.

The fundamental point I would like to make here is that public criticism of public spending of all kinds—including my kind of rhetoric—needs to be more vigorously answered. No one has a God-given right to public funds. If the people getting public money can't defend their use of it, they shouldn't get it.

I admit the fight may not be fair; I admit the wrong side may occasionally win. This is an old and very difficult problem. The bromide, "Whoever knew truth to be bested by falsehood in a fair fight?" is tellingly answered by John Stuart Mill in his great "Essay on Liberty." Mill points out that the whole history of mankind seems to be largely a history of falsehood kicking the living daylights out of truth. He reminds us that Socrates was put to death because his truth was called impious—another way of saying inconvenient for the establishment. And Jesus, who has been worshiped by a goodly proportion of humankind for 2000 years, was crucified for speaking the truth that love is the salvation of mankind.

Mill concedes that truth crushed to earth may rise and rise again until it wins out. But that can take a long, long time, and the false can plague men's decisions for years, even centuries.

How can we reconcile the possibility that criticism may suppress and crush the truth seekers of this world with the need to expose and reduce a waste of federal resources that goes against the public weal?

The answer is discussion and debate—open, free, and as vigorous as possible. The wise and articulate professors at the great University of Wisconsin should not fear that. They are not being asked to drink hemlock. They are not being crucified on even a figurative cross. They are simply being challenged to justify and to defend on their own terms the expenditure of thousands of the public's hard-earned tax dollars.

Some of those on the receiving end of the Golden Fleece awards *have* fought back, I am delighted to say. Their retaliation has been colorful, hard-hitting, and occasionally even hurt a little. Here are a few of the zingers we got in return.

Golden Hypocrisy Award

The mayor of Salt Lake City was so perturbed about an award we gave to the Department of the Interior for spending more than $140,000 on a wave-making machine for his city's swimming pool that he ribbed me for using a shower every day in the locker room that is provided for senators on the ground floor of the Senate Office Building. He estimated an annual maintenance of that locker room at $200,000. (The actual cost is probably 10 percent of that.) Since I happen to jog five miles to work every morning, I take a shower there. The mayor figured that only about fifteen senators use the locker room (he was generous there —probably only five or six use it) and, by allocating the cost of the facility to each of the users on a pro-rata basis and concluding that I must take a couple of hundred showers a year, he computed my shower cost to the federal government as $12.35 each.

The mayor may have a point except that I've been consistently opposed to the extravagant installation. Moreover, if I stopped using it, there would be no savings at all, and the atmosphere of my office, not to mention the floor of the Senate, would deteriorate considerably, especially on a hot summer day.

Earth Is Flat Award

After we gave out a Fleece to the space agency for proposing to spend more than $14 million for a seven-year search for extraterrestrial intelligence, the astronomers at a meeting of the American Association for the Advancement of Science made me an honorary member of the Flat Earth Society.

Dr. Frank Drake of Cornell University added a little footnote: "When Columbus left Spain, there was no evidence that the New World existed, let alone Wisconsin. Even if we discover a dead civilization, the information they leave us could in a week surpass everything in the Library of Congress." They might have subtitled my honor as the Columbus-Would-Still-Be-in-Port-if-Proxmire-Had-His-Way Award.

Golden Sheep Drop Award

This award was bestowed on me by Donald Morris, a columnist for the *Houston Post,* who was also in a high dudgeon about my lack of gung ho for extraterrestrial communication.

> This column herewith establishes a Golden Sheep Drop Award which will be conferred from time to time on a member of the

legislative branch who has taken the cheapest shot at the easiest target for the purpose of getting his name in the media. The first award, a triple life-size, handsomely mounted specimen, goes to the foremost master of the cheap shot, William Proxmire, himself.

Even this knee in the groin had its distinction. After all, it was something to be the *first* recipient. And if you're going to be called a cheap-shot artist, it's nice to be called a master.

Golden Hide Award

The reaction to our award of a Fleece of the Month to the U.S. Treasury for the favoritism they exhibited by giving tax breaks to Americans living abroad, including the exemption of the first $20,000 of income (how would you like *that* exemption for yourself?) led to the receipt in my office of a raunchy, smelly, bedraggled camel's hide of a sickening brown hue. With it came a plaque reading: GOLDEN HIDE AWARD PRESENTED TO SENATOR WILLIAM PROXMIRE BY THE AMERICANS IN THE NORTHERN UNITED ARAB EMIRATES.

In my more than twenty years in the Senate I have found that, without question, the deepest resentment is provoked when a tax privilege is threatened. In this case *all* Americans living overseas were given the first-$20,000-of-income exemption. It is true that some Americans overseas work under conditions of considerable hardship. But the income tax exemption is given to U.S. citizens in Paris or Monte Carlo or Rome or the beautiful South Sea isles as well as to those who labor in a hot and barren desert. Why should they get it? There's no exemption for the Kentucky coal miner, the Brooklyn garbage collector, the Wisconsin foundry worker, all of whom labor under conditions of dust, noise, heat, smell, and muscular strain that you wouldn't believe without experiencing, and pay a full tax on every nickel they make.

We got another award for our tax exemption plea. The citation read as follows:

To William Proxmire, for his brilliant fantasy entitled "Americans Abroad," adapted from F. Scott Fitzgerald, starring the courageous legislator who tracks down and eliminates the last of the dissolute breed of mink-swathed and roulette-playing expatriates.

We never received the prize, but it was described as a handsome pair of clay feet mounted on a marble base. The work was said to have been done by a well-known American sculptor living in Paris.

The Fleece may have made enemies but it has also made friends. And one of the most encouraging developments is that the spirit is catching. There have been offshoot awards made— some similar, some identical, and some approaching the problem of extravagant spending in other ways.

For instance, Peter Peyser, a bright young New York congressman, has started a regular monthly Monkey Wrench Award. His first one went to the Department of Agriculture for regulations that required the mailing of forms *every month* to the households of 5 million families receiving food stamps. As Peyser pointed out, the cost of the mailing was more than $1 million a month. But food stamp recipients are required to reaffirm their eligibility only every *three* months, which means that eight of the yearly mailings have no purpose whatsoever and are merely thrown away. By eliminating these 40 million letters, more than $8 million would be saved.

Senator James Sasser of Tennessee is another young legislator who has worked very hard to expose and reduce waste in the federal government. At his suggestion, the General Accounting Office (GAO) installed a toll-free nationwide hotline to help citizens fight fraud, abuse, and mismanagement in our government.

Sasser described a few typical cases: A government contractor takes materials from a government facility for personal use; federal grants in a multi-county area are being mismanaged; or test equipment belonging to the TVA is being converted improperly to private use.

The hotline was a smash success from the beginning. In the first month there were over 4000 telephone calls. In the category of the constantly trickling faucet of waste through picayune but genuine dishonesty, a case turned up involving a government car. A service station attendant, conniving with the driver, had been filling out credit card claims for $15 to $20 worth of gas but pumping no gas. The driver would give the attendant $5 and keep $10 or $15 himself. As Sasser pointed out, if all the gas bills were averaged out with the mileage figure on the car, it was getting about two miles to the gallon.

The GAO has reported that a surprising 50 percent or more of the calls on the Sasser hotline have been substantial enough to warrant follow-ups.

In Wisconsin two state legislators, William Rogers and David Berger, established the Rose and Ragweed Awards to praise efficient tax-saving performances and to expose waste. The Rose Award went to one official for providing information to stop "double dipping" by state employees and to another official for cutting the costs of operating the state examining boards.

The Ragweed Award was given to an official who spent $4000 of public money for new office furniture.

A Golden Fleece—Kansas Style was started in 1979 by State Representatives Charles Laird and Anthony Hensley. They didn't mince words. Their awards are designed to bring to the public eye those "who are guilty of ripping off the Kansas taxpayer, including fellow legislators, lobbyists, city and county commissioners, school boards, school administrators and judges. We don't want to leave out anybody."

The first award went to the president of Kansas State University for "fixing up his office to the tune of $100,000" with state money. Then, for good measure, they tossed in two runners-up.

1. All the contractors who have done shoddy work for the state during the past few years, e.g. the new K.U. Law School building completed last year that now has cracks in it. Roofs at KNI in Topeka that leak and get the little kids wet who live in the building.

Contractors at Wichita State who built the Learning Resources Center, the one that now has bricks falling off the sides and concrete deteriorating.

2. The Ferro Corporation of Golden, Colorado and the Kansas D.O.T. The Corporation received $422,000 to put plastic thermal stripes on streets in Topeka. The stripes were supposed to last 3 to 5 years; now, 9 months after they were applied many of the stripes have vanished.

Senator Bill Roth, the conscientious, economy-minded senator from Delaware, has developed another variation: he has organized a bipartisan task force, including Senators Chafee, Danforth, Lugar, Nunn, Stone, and me, committed to the proposition to bring before the Senate specific proposals to reduce federal spending and to put the Senate on record again and again on the economy issue.

We call ourselves the S.O.B.'s or Save Our Bucks.

This S.O.B. initiative has resulted in the Senate's cutting out a solid $1.3 billion from the 1979 budget: $144 million from the Treasury–Post Office–White House appropriation, $178 million from the State Justice Commerce appropriation, $50 million from the Legislative appropriation, $810 million from the Housing and Urban appropriation, and $126.5 million from the Agriculture appropriation.

Senator Roth has organized colorful press conferences, equipping members of his task force with such items as pencils with erasers at both ends and no lead in between so that dollars can only be eliminated, not added, and with knives to slash the budget and visors to shield weary eyes during long hours of painstakingly picking out the fat and waste while leaving the vital, necessary substance.

GAO—A Good Watchdog

As a taxpayer, you are fortunate to have the General Accounting Office (GAO) working for you. The GAO serves as a congressional watchdog over the programs on which we spend your money. It is headed by a comptroller general and manned by some 4000 expert accountants and auditors. For more than twenty years I have used this agency to investigate allegations of our federal government's waste, mismanagement, and loopholes for fraud, not only in this country but all over the world.

My experience with the GAO has been consistently good. Their findings have been generally admitted even by the agencies they criticize. They are remarkably accurate. They have saved this nation billions of dollars. Recently they made an estimate of the cost of the waste and fraud which plagues our government. (The estimates, of course, did not include expenditure of funds that are failing to meet their intended purpose, which I will deal with in a later chapter.) But consider their findings in the limited area of fraud alone.

On September 18, 1978, the GAO reported on a possible $250 billion of our federal resources "susceptible to fraud and other white collar crimes." In their conclusion, they state: "No one knows the extent of fraud against the government, but Department of Justice officials believe it ranges from $2.5 billion to $25 billion a year."

Yet fraud is very likely the smallest part of the waste of taxpayers' dollars.

As many forces push, and will continue to push, for increased government spending, and with this spending take a mammoth 40 percent of personal income out of your pockets, many more recruits are needed for economy campaigns of all kinds and descriptions.

(4)

Big Brass Rip-offs

ONE OF THE MOST insidious temptations for those in high office is to turn on the spigot for their own benefit, using the old, tired argument that whatever it is, it's only a tiny part of the enormous federal budget. Or, that with all the heavy responsibilities we bear, the taxpayer should be happy to toss us a few thousand just for fun. I have a collection of interesting headlines bearing on this fun at your expense.

*

THE NAVY FLIES 64 AIRCRAFT AND 1,334 RESERVE OFFICERS TO LAS VEGAS FOR A REUNION OF THE TAILHOOK ASSOCIATION

The dateline was September 6, 1974, at the height of the energy shortage.

The Tailhook Association is a private, nongovernmental organization composed of active duty, reserve, and retired military pilots and civilians interested in aircraft carrier affairs.

The flights cost more than $191,000 and used up 347,000 gallons of fuel. They were authorized by the chief of Naval Operations and justified on the books as "space required" travel, though none of the officers carried the required documentation for space-required travel, which means transportation during a temporary or permanent change of station. It was, I suppose, a fairly typical subterfuge.

Many aircraft were taken off operational duty for this mass

junket, including C–9, C–118, C–117, and CT–39 transports; trainers; A–7 and F–4 fighters; and the VIP planes designated C–131 and TA–3. A number were one-way flights; several of them forced the cancellation of planned training exercises.

The airlift was of such magnitude that it required the assignment of thirteen navy personnel for ground support and administration.

About 1600 personnel attended the reunion. There were 6 vice admirals, 16 rear admirals, 69 captains, 1063 other officers, 2 enlisted men, 40 naval reservists, 164 navy retirees, 69 active duty Marines, 7 retired Marines, 17 federally employed civilians, and 153 nongovernment civilians.

Planes left for Las Vegas from California, Washington, D.C., Florida, Texas, Mississippi, Louisiana, Virginia, Nebraska, Maryland, Pennsylvania, Arizona, and from one aircraft carrier, the *Coral Sea.*

Only seven months later, in April 1975, a group of 400 air force officers, called the Red River Valley Fighter Pilots Association and nicknamed River Rats, also held a social gathering in Las Vegas.

The officers of this private organization told GAO investigators that no government transportation was used for this reunion except for the transporting of an air force general who was the guest speaker. However, the GAO found a number of flights into nearby air force installations that carried officers attending the party.

The River Rats refused to provide details to the GAO and blocked entrance to the meeting for "security reasons." The air force refused to provide details because they considered the River Rats a private organization.

When we are told it will take weeks to reinforce our troops in Europe by air, there is great comfort in knowing that the navy and air force can airlift thousands of officers to Las Vegas. Where there's a will, there's a way.

Such an utter disregard for tax dollars and for a fuel energy crisis can only be described as calculated stupidity. Perhaps the Chief of Naval Operations should be provided with an "I am fuelish" button!

*

THE NAVY EXPLODES $15,000 INTO $500,000 TO FANCY UP MANSION FOR THE VEEP

Public Law 93-346, passed in July 1974, designated a navy-owned house in Washington as the "official temporary residence of the Vice-President of the United States." The word *temporary* was added because other legislation had been passed authorizing a future permanent residence for Veeps. The law gave the Navy Department responsibility for staffing, care, maintenance, repair, improvement, alteration, and furnishing the official residence, subject to the supervision and control of then Vice-President Rockefeller.

I opposed this bill on the Senate floor, but lost, after assurances were given that nothing elaborate was contemplated—only necessary refurbishing—and that the cost would be about $15,000.

Instead of this modest sum, the navy, through the Executive Office of the President, asked for and received $537,000 for "necessary" refurbishing, to wit:

$41,000 for furniture
33,000 for miscellaneous items such as linen, silverware chests, and accessories
26,400 for drapes
21,200 for silverware
18,100 for carpets
10,400 for china
4,900 for crystal

In addition, the navy planned to spend $170,000 to replace window air conditioners with a central unit.

*

WHITE HOUSE CALLS FOR GOVERNMENT AUSTERITY AS WHITE
HOUSE SPENDING SOARS

Americans follow the first family and their doings in the White
House every day in newspapers, on television, and on radio. We
praise or criticize, laugh or groan at what goes on at the top of
the government. Our own conduct is influenced constantly by
what the President says, but probably much more by what he
does. Especially when he says one thing and does another.

When he says the way to fight inflation is to be careful about
expenditures and to save, we listen, but when he increases spending in the White House itself people in and out of government
are likely to go and do likewise.

In December of 1975 I gave the White House a Fleece for its
efforts to add to its empire through increased funds while calling
for austerity from the rest of the government. However, through
a series of little-noted actions the increases were accomplished:

- The White House dramatically upped funding for "consultants"
  from the initial $350,000 in the fiscal year 1968 to a whopping
  $3,850,000 in fiscal year 1976. This was an increase of $1.6 million
  since the advent of President Ford, when the total was already
  $2,250,000.
- During the same year, 1976, the White House requested a 100
  percent supplement for the discretionary contingency fund,
  founded for "unanticipated needs." The appropriation grew from
  $500,000 in 1975 to $1 million. In the past such funds had been
  limited to support various executive office activities and commis-
  sions. But in 1976 they could be used for any activity—at home
  or abroad—which the President designated as a "furtherance of
  national interest."
- In 1975, without any legislative authorization, travel funds for the
  White House staff (*not* the President) were increased from
  $40,000 to $100,000, or by 150 percent.
- In 1975 the White House had 54 aides earning between $37,500
  and $44,600 a year. In 1976 they asked authority from Congress
  to hire an unlimited number of these high-level employees. The

House of Representatives opposed the idea and placed a ceiling of 95 on the number of executive-level positions. This amounted to an addition of 41 positions.

• Under a bill proposed by the Office of the White House, travel funds and funds for official receptions, entertainment, and representation would continue to be exempt from audit by the General Accounting Office.

• To add insult to injury, the White House insisted on a provision in H.R. 8617, the bill to amend the Hatch Act, which would exempt all White House personnel (about 500) and those on special assignments to the White House (about 80 in 1975) from that article in the Hatch Act which prohibits government employees from engaging in "political activity" while on duty, while in a government building, or while wearing a uniform.

*

ENERGY CZAR CONSUMES 19,000 GALLONS OF FUEL JETTING AROUND THE COUNTRY URGING ECONOMY IN ENERGY CONSUMPTION

That's no wild headline but a fact. Frank Zarb, as head of the Federal Energy Administration, spent $35,000 chartering airplanes during ten months of 1975 for trips to various American cities to convince local business or civic groups to save fuel. He made thirteen trips in all, and for eight of them he used a plush air force four-engine jet which burned enough energy in an hour to supply the average American driver with gas for a year.

Mr. Zarb was a hard-working, conscientious administrator. He failed, however, to see the irony of indulging in a private plane at the very time he was preaching economy.

On his trip to Little Rock, Arkansas, he burned more than 2500 gallons of jet fuel and his flight cost the federal government $3053. In Little Rock he urged Americans, according to the *Arkansas Democrat,* to end "their romance with the chrome-plated gunboat," that is, the luxury car that was a status symbol for half a century.

His first scheduled event in Little Rock was set for 5:30 P.M.

A direct commercial flight was scheduled to leave Washington Airport at 12:55 local time and arrive at 3:10 Little Rock time. The cost of the round-trip charter was twenty times greater than the round-trip commercial coach fare.

Mr. Zarb was asked to give the commencement address and receive an honorary degree at Hofstra University's Business School in New York City. There are commercial flights between Washington and New York every hour on the hour from 7:00 A.M. to 10:00 P.M. every day. But he felt moved to charter a flight to La Guardia at the government's extra expense.

His flight in an air force jet to Jackson, Mississippi, on April 10 cost the government $3199 and used up approximately 2600 gallons of fuel. He told the Mississippi Economic Council that Americans were going to have become more efficient in conserving automobile, home heating, and industrial fuel so that the country could curtail oil imports sharply over the next three years. He left Washington at 9:00 A.M. and arrived back at 7:30 P.M. He could have arisen a little earlier and caught a commercial plane leaving at 7:55 A.M. at the National Airport. True, he wouldn't have arrived home until 9:55 P.M. But the savings on the ticket alone would have been over $3000, not to speak of the fuel waste.

When he spoke to the National Rural Electric Cooperative Association on January 21, 1975, Mr. Zarb said, according to the *Times Picayune,* that "everyone will have to give up something" under the energy program.

It may seem unfair to single out Frank Zarb for wasting, as energy czar, both fuel energy and government money. For as a matter of fact there exists a $66 million fleet of twenty-three luxurious air force jets standing by solely to transport top government officials to the ends of the earth at a cost to the taxpayers of over $6 million a year.

That little-known executive airline is called the 89th Military Airlift Wing (Special Missions) and is based at Andrews Air Force Base near Washington, D.C. I awarded the Fleece of the

Year to the air force for this plush service, but in all justice it should be shared by all the government big shots who insist on such special treatment.

In the first ten months of 1975, the 89th made 875 flights carrying government officials as passengers, at a cost of over $6 million. Not surprisingly, 87 percent of these flights were taken by high-ranking defense brass or those requesting Defense Department flights.

Other departments and agencies have used these executive jets often, the Treasury Department heading the list in 1975 with sixty-seven flights. The high figure results from the activities of Secretary William Simon who, according to air force records, took fifty-eight flights during the first ten months of 1975 at a government cost of $328,784, which averages out to $5669 a flight. William Clements, Howard Callaway, Frank Zarb, Henry Kissinger, and William Middendorf were also frequent users of this fleet of planes that is on call twenty-four hours a day for top brass. All they have to do is call up and request a flight.

These planes should not be confused with the presidential aircraft, also based at Andrews, or with the 150 or so "administrative support" aircraft sitting on military facilities throughout the world to transport high-ranking officials.

The aircraft are outfitted in a special VIP configuration— hence the *V* in their type designations. Three jet VC–137$8$B planes have a capacity of about fifty, and they go all the way to the two-prop VC–6As with a capacity of about five people.

This fleet costs Uncle Sam $55.7 million; operation costs run from $2206 an hour for the biggest to $155 an hour for the smallest.

The VC–137Bs and VC–135Bs (similar to the Boeing 707) have sleeping facilities for ten persons. Military aides who accompany the passengers on these flights to serve food and drink and assist in other ways are justified by the air force as necessary for passenger safety. These men are called Air Passenger Specialists.

The stupidity of this massive airlift is that, in almost every case, commercial flights are available to the same destination. Using them would not only save the government hundreds of thousands of dollars; they would also have helped the then depressed U.S. airline industry.

This exclusive fleet has gone to every point in the globe— Middle East, South America, Europe, the Far East, and the USSR. Except for White House trips, costs of non–Defense Department flights are reimbursed from agency funds.

A table indicating the number of flights taken by department or agency brass from January to October of 1975 follows.

Agency/Department	Number of Flights
Defense Department	849
(Roughly 100 of these congressional)	
Treasury	67
State	26
Federal Energy Administration	11
Energy Research and Development	8
NASA	6
Corps of Engineers	1
FBI	1
Agriculture	1
Secret Service	1
Interior ,	1

Note: This chart is computed from detailed raw air force flight data and may reflect a small degree of scheduling error.

Two years later, in November of 1977, we found that the use of government aircraft had shot up alarmingly. According to an internal Department of Defense (DOD) audit, military planes have been exploited by civilian VIPs with a cost to the taxpayer of at least $52.3 million. They have been systematically misused for low-priority missions—administrative support or purely personal flights—instead of for combat training, and, in many, many cases, when commercial transportation was available and of course much cheaper.

What we got from the DOD audit was the picture of every high-ranking officer or civilian in the Pentagon free to request special transportation simply on the basis of rank. The audit also puts the lie to the age-old excuse that special handling of generals and admirals is appropriate because the aircraft have to fly anyway and there is no additional cost if the brass go along. In fact the whole thing is very costly: extra aircraft must be on hand and, with such extensive use of pilots for ferrying VIPs, the training of men for wartime missions suffers. With high-ranking passengers on board the pilots cannot conduct multiple landings, high-ceiling penetrations, simulated emergency operations, single-engine landings, and other exercises for preparedness.

The Defense Department auditors (Defense Audit Service) should get a commendation for uncovering this exploitation of government aircraft for nonessential purposes. Here are some of the facts.

An audit of army executive and support flights found them not cost effective compared to available commercial transportation. At one command alone, 119 support aircraft valued at $24.9 million would no longer be required if current cost-effective standards were applied.

The air force systematically used (as of November 1977) 104 T-39 jet aircraft, designed originally for wartime readiness, as support aircraft instead—at a cost of $26 million in excess flying time and 24 million gallons of wasted aviation fuel. And the pilots were being used to fly so many administrative support missions that they were not getting their required readiness training accomplished. When told by the secretary of defense to cut down on the number of flights for the Pentagon, Congress, and VIPs from the executive branch, the air force simply transferred several of their unused craft to "administrative support" in another part of the country, even though this was contrary to the secretary's instructions.

The Navy and Marine Corps operate, for high-ranking brass, a semiregular helicopter taxi service between Norfolk, Virginia, and Washington, D.C., that duplicates regular commercial service between these points at a much higher cost.

A review of 6000 Navy and Marine Corps flights at six locations found that 1500 of these did not even carry passengers on official business. The helicopters at Quantico Marine Base were a good example of this exploitation—they were simply a taxi service between the Pentagon, Andrews, Norfolk, Philadelphia, and Quantico.

There are 18,000 active aircraft and helicopters in the U.S. arsenal. Eleven thousand two hundred of these are support aircraft or transports. That leaves only 6800 for combat aircraft.

It's time to place first things first. Wartime readiness training should come before the indulgences and luxuries offered as a matter of course to more and more government employees who have easily learned to "pull rank"—but not to count the cost.

Deep within the Pentagon's budget lies a little-noticed item called "Emergencies and Extraordinary Expenses." It is part of the huge operation-and-maintenance fund to keep aircraft flying and ships sailing. It is divided into two parts and indeed one of these parts has to do with classified military functions. The other part might be titled "Hidden Fund to Wine and Dine American and Foreign VIPs."

The Pentagon's party fund is used for a wide variety of travel and entertainment. It pays for unreimbursed congressional trips, receptions for foreign military leaders, welcoming parties and going-away parties for the Pentagon hierarchy, flowers, corsages, gifts, and tea parties for wives, boat cruises, conferences, lunches, dinners, change of command ceremonies, and bulk purchases of alcoholic beverages.

This is an "extraordinary" fund, but there is nothing of an "emergency" nature about it. No last-minute crisis—these social events are planned far in advance. What is extraordinary is that it amounts to around $1.2 million.

Out of that sum, reported to have been spent in twelve months (dates vary by service), the air force accounted for $408,946, the army $357,00, the navy $286,265, and the Office of the Secretary of Defense/Joint Chiefs/Defense Agencies together used $160,992.

These moneys have traditionally been exploited. A minor but telling example is that of the retiring official who was given a party *by* his colleagues, with expenses of $176 charged to the Pentagon budget; then, a few days later, he gave a party *for* his friends at a cost of $271.80, also charged to the taxpayer.

Larger farewell parties for top officials often run to thousands of dollars. The entertainment of foreign visitors is an enormous item on the list. Every reception for any group— military or civilian—is paid for out of Emergencies and Extraordinary Expenses. Congressional travel may top the list, and I believe Congress should share with the Pentagon this Fleece Award.

One small jotting intrigues me: Former Deputy-Secretary Clements, a multimillionaire, was reimbursed $8 for porter service in New Orleans.

Some of the most elaborate entertaining is for visiting military leaders from other countries. Each trip costs, on average, about $2000. Meanwhile, our overseas officials are also running up huge entertainment bills. The competition for big spending is close between our representatives to the SALT talks, the Mutual Balanced Force Reduction talks, and the Law of the Seas Conference.

The Department of Defense (DOD) has elaborate internal regulations aimed at how their "extraordinary" money shall be spent. According to Directive 7250.13, they "will be used to maintain the standing and prestige of the United States." There are ratios for the number of non-DOD guests to be entertained. Regulations establish a list of items that cannot be paid for by the government, and then immediately make exceptions to such restrictions. Retirement ceremonies, for example, are not covered (*except* where approved in advance); expenses for conferences, conventions, and working groups are not approved (*except* where approved in advance); gifts, mementos, and calling cards are not approved (*except* for wreaths, nominal-cost mementos, and others approved in advance).

As a matter of practice, therefore, these restrictions are hollow and meaningless. All sorts of ceremonies are funded; self-entertainment is allowed frequently and at great expense; receptions during conferences and conventions and working group meetings are common.

What should be done about this abuse of entertainment spending? Obviously some entertaining for diplomatic purposes is necessary. But I am convinced that we are being foolishly profligate in performance of our duty "to maintain the standing and prestige of the United States."

Moreover, all these party funds should not be hidden in the budget side by side with classified military defense needs. They should be identified frankly. *And* reduced drastically!

The following list speaks for itself. It represents the fiscal year 1977 Emergencies and Extraordinary Expenses Account. Technically, there are four budget items, one for the Office of the Secretary of Defense (OSD)/Joint Chiefs (JCS)/Defense Agencies, and three others for army, navy, and air force—all in the operations and maintenance function.

OSD/JCS/Defense Agencies

Stag reception for the German armament director	$363.00
Stag dinner for Ambassador Robert Strausz-Hupe	$178.59
Boat cruise and picnic for foreign officials	$173.00
Luncheon and flowers for General Toufanian's wife	$129.00
Tea party for wives of the Standing Consultative Committee at SALT	$107.00
Replenishment of gifts for the Secretary of Defense to give away	$1660.32
Dinner for the Defense Science Board	$967.00
Reception for the Reserve Force Policy Board	$850.00
Functions hosted by the Defense Mapping Agency at the International Hydrographic Organization in Monaco	$700.00
A party given *for* Dr. Walter LaBerge, Assistant Secretary for Defense Support NATO *by* his colleagues	$176.00

A party given *by* Dr. Walter LaBerge *for* his colleagues	$271.80
Various hotel bills for the Secretary of Defense on overseas trips	$1280.00
Social functions at the National War College	$2000.00
Air transportation from Capetown to Bloemfontein for Mrs. Gatewood, wife of the Republic of South Africa Naval Attaché, who was joining an attaché tour arranged by the South African Defense Force for foreign attachés and their wives	$139.42
Secret entertainment by the National Security Agency	$12,161.74
Luncheon in honor of the representatives attending the Four Nations Digital Radar Landmass Simulation Conference in Rome	$100.00
Change of command ceremonies for retiring general and flag rank officers.	$474.42
Luncheon and dedication of the Uniformed Services University of the Health Sciences	$718.00
Luncheon and dinner for Board of Regents of the University	$370.00
Cocktail and dinner party for officials of the Four Power Armament Directors' meeting in Bonn	$484.79
1977 Annual Supergrade Conference expenses	$891.40
Reception for representatives to U.S.–Micronesia consultations	$500.00
Reception for Minister of Defense of Israel	$9879.00
Bouquets, flowers, corsages	$166.25
Farewell dinner for Secretary Rumsfeld, Deputy Secretaries Clements and Ellsworth.	$1992.00
Five custom-made cakes and checkroom services for farewell reception for Secretary Rumsfeld	$507.00
Porter fees for Deputy Secretary Clements in New Orleans	$8.00
Refreshments for congressional staffs and press corps, January 15, 1977	$149.50
Dinner honoring distinguished guests attending UN Regional Cartographic Conference in Bangkok, Thailand, January 17, 1977	$200.00
Purchase of alcoholic beverages, "to be used in connection with representational functions to promote U.S. national interests"	$485.34
Preholiday commanders' reception for "prominent officials and members of the Philadelphia Industrial Community"	$975.00
Commanders' reception for "local dignitaries" in Richmond, Va.	$604.00

Army

Annual luncheon for spouses of civilian aides to the Secretary of the Army	$387.14
Reception for unveiling painting honoring the 442nd Regimental Combat Team	$68.00
Exemption requested for hosting the 149th Meeting of the Permanent Joint Board on Defense, Canada-U.S.	$3400.00
Monthly vouchers for entertaining congressional aides; average about	$400.00
Army commanders' dinner, October 3, 1977; cost at least	$1100.00
Party for Congressional Committee staff and Congressional Budget Office staff.	$468.76
Reception for civilian aides and Secretariat Alumni Conference (includes reception, badges, luncheons, dinners, ceremonies)	$7108.77
Reception by Office of Chief of Public Affairs, New York branch, for the press	$299.00
Proposed for June 30, 1978: Requested exemption for costs of reception following retirement review in honor of General Walter T. Kerwin	

Navy

Reception on 201st birthday of U.S. Navy	$2808.00
Dinner for Comptroller of the Navy	$666.15
Dinner for consular corps on 201st birthday of the Marine Corps	$1000.00
Reception for guests attending commissioning of the USS *Los Angeles*	$1200.00
Reception, dinner, and ball to honor non-DOD guests on 201st birthday of the U.S. Marine Corps	$2540.38
Reception in honor of the Assistant Secretary of the Army	$2556.32
Reception to honor state and city officials in Philadelphia	$684.08
Dinner in honor of local Memphis, Tennessee, officials (DOD personnel paid their own costs; civilians charged to government)	$1680.00
Dinner in honor of Navy Oceanographic Advisory Committee	$450.00
Breakfast to honor certain civilian officials during the annual American Bar Association meeting	$452.40
Reception in honor of the Virginia Supreme Court, Norfolk City Council, and presidents of local business leagues	$828.00
Reception in honor of the Commandant of the Marine Corps and community leaders at Camp Lejeune	$1566.62

Reception to honor local civil and business leaders in the
  Philadelphia area $2370.25

Air Force

Lunch at La Bagatelle for Brazilian military representatives	$335.00
Dinner by Secretary Stetson for General McBride	$1180.05
Purchase of confiscated beverages	$49.52
Visit of Colonel General Cemalovic of Yugoslavia (the general was given tours and briefings on the B–1 bomber, F–16, and AMST)	$3410.37
Reception for Air Force Board for Correction of Military Records (Secretary Stetson by memo states this will be the last time he will approve this expenditure)	$324.30
Party at Andrews Air Force Base Officers Club for Colonel Arbe, Air Attaché, Embassy of Uruguay	$195.68
Reception for Scientific Advisory Board, fall general meeting	$1453.59
Luncheon at Watergate Terrace in honor of Colonel Shport, Air Attaché, USSR	$82.95
Visit of Commander Colombian Air Force; dinners, lunches, transportation, golf, laundry, flowers	$2077.32
Reception in honor of Secretary of Air Force John C. Stetson.	$2320.82
Visit of Commander of Bolivian Air Force	$2892.36
Visit of Commander, Mexican Air Force, including a visit to Disneyland	$3284.19
Books, stamp plaques, medallions for Secretary Stetson's trip to the Middle East, including an eagle weathervane.	$861.41
Reception honoring the Corps of Air Attachés	$6471.00
Reception for Assistant Secretary of the Air Force	$334.75
Farewell dinner for Brigadier General Temporini of Argentina	$357.24
Visit by Chief of Staff, Kuwait Armed Forces	$4197.34
Reception for Air Force Historical Advisory Committee	$221.80
Expenses incurred in connection with USAF Independence Day Air Attaché Golf Tournament (trophies, greens fees, reception)	$3352.91
Walnut plaque purchases	$2158.60

A Stronger and Leaner Military

Unfortunately we don't live in a Sunday school world where all
we have to do is love our Soviet neighbor and he will love us

back. We face a tough, disciplined dictatorship—the world's second largest economy controlled by a clique who preach world revolution by force and, if necessary, violence.

Of course we should try our best to reason and negotiate with this adversary. But our strongest ally in this sincere drive for peace must be a strong military force and one that does not come at bargain-basement prices. Military spending will cost us tens of billions of dollars for many years to come.

Our military should be stronger than it is. It also should be lean and mean, not soft and fat.

It should not waste money. Did you know that there are more civilians working for the Defense Department than for all the other agencies of government combined, if you leave out the Postal Service? There are nearly one million civilians —almost as many employed now as there were at the height of the Vietnam War in 1969, when combat forces were nearly twice as large. We simply don't need that many bureaucrats. The Pentagon could save more than a billion dollars by simply discharging 10 percent of them and, in my opinion, they should do so now.

With such a colossal bureaucracy, wasted time turns into millions of wasted man-days, and the Parkinson law of busy work of any kind to fill an idle hour becomes painfully real. A minor incident illustrates this.

From time to time the USAF Uniform Board has been asked if it were proper for male uniformed air force gentlemen to carry umbrellas. The answer always came back no. It was deemed unprofessional and bad for the air force image.

But the question persisted. Why can't we? So the Air Force Uniform Board decided to conduct an umbrella test. The plan went up the chain of command and was approved by a general officer. The test was scheduled for a six-month period between November 1, 1978, and April 30, 1979.

An announcement went forth to all USAF male personnel in the Pentagon. For six months you may use an umbrella if you want—nothing outrageous, just a standard black or blue commercial model.

Meanwhile the planners had been busy developing a survey of a random sample of 1700 male Pentagonians. Research experts in the air force personnel office were confident this survey would be 95 percent reliable, and on March 1, 1979, it was sent out to the 1700 randomly selected males.

The package contained a covering page explaining the purpose and giving mailing instructions. A foreword, a Privacy Act statement, and advice on filling out the questionnaire were included.

What did the air force want to know? Such burning facts as: frequency of umbrella use; was it used with a raincoat?; comments on its use by military and civilian personnel; did it interfere with saluting and other military courtesies?; did it seem to reduce professional image?; female air force reaction; did it detract from the combat-ready image?; recommended types of umbrellas; freedom of choice on use; problems with the design or style of umbrellas.

The survey responses were fed into a computer. Then the staff experts sorted out the major conclusions. A recommendation went to the USAF Uniform Board, which reached a decision and passed it up the chain of command to the Air Force Chief of Staff.

The cost was recorded as $3104.

*

The Russians have been criticized for having three men in supply and support for every one they have in combat-ready positions. How many do we have in supply and support? We have *ten* for every soldier, sailor, Marine, or airman that we have trained for combat. This is what is known as a *sluggish logistic tail.* With personnel costs a massive 58 percent of all military costs, we could save hundreds of millions, *and* have a more effective force, by reducing that luxurious supply and support burden.

It is a common misconception that women can't improve the

performance or reduce the cost of military personnel. They can. One of the few changes in the military in recent years that has measurably improved our armed forces is the enlistment of more women. Women military personnel have higher education requirements and they increase the IQ and the general intellectual status; they are absent from work and training less often than men, and this includes time lost because of pregnancy. They are less prone to alcoholism and drug abuse or just plain AWOL. Also women military personnel cost less because they have fewer dependents and are more likely to stay in the army, navy, or air force after they are trained.

Except in the area of muscular strength and endurance, women perform as well as men. President Eisenhower's observation has been confirmed. He admitted that before World War II he thought there was no place for women in the army. But as supreme commander of our troops in Europe, he found that women significantly improved the performance of our armed forces during that war.

One of the factors adding to our military expense is the *grade creep*. We can save millions by limited promotions. Today we have the ridiculous situation of having more generals in the army and more admirals in the navy than we had at the height of World War II when there existed six times as many soldiers and sailors to command. My staff has made a projection that by the year 2000 everyone in the army will be a general and everyone in the navy an admiral. If you want secure careers for your children send them all into the military.

The higher status an officer enjoys before he (or she) retires, the more retirement pay is donated. Military personnel can opt out after twenty years (at the age of forty or so) and the half pay can go on a long time. Or after thirty years, when they're only fifty or so, they can receive a juicy two-thirds pay. That retirement cost continues to climb as more and more officers are promoted beyond any reason for their rank except the money cushion.

The cost of all this to the long-suffering taxpayer is of course immense.

Military Procurement Waste

If you sat down and tried to design a system guaranteed to waste money, you couldn't do any better than our military procurement program—the defense contract racket. In the private sector, the economic system balances itself out because firms are rewarded by higher profits if they hold costs down, watch every nickel, and get as much work per hour as they can out of their work force. They also acquire labor-saving equipment that pays for itself in a few years and keeps costs down, which is the key to a successful operation.

In defense contracting the system works precisely in reverse. The higher your costs, the higher your profits. In 1976 the Defense Department introduced a new profit system designed to provide incentives for contractors to use more labor-saving equipment to keep their costs down. The idea was great; the result was a flat failure because the Defense Department made investment in such equipment a feeble 10 percent factor in computing allowable profits, and cost (of labor and materials) was weighted at a heavy 50 percent. It was still the same game: the higher the cost the higher the profits.

After a thorough investigation, the GAO concluded that the new system had increased neither investment nor productivity, nor reduced costs, and that the $200 million of additional profits in the second year after the program was installed simply enriched defense contractors at the expense of the government with no improvement—*none*—in contractor performance.

The answer is to insist on more fixed-price contracts, without loopholes for cost increases. The Congress should simply refuse to fund weapon systems until we know the price and it is guaranteed that the contractor will be made to stick to it, precisely as contractors do in the private sector. This would give the incentive for the contractor to hold his costs down, and American industry can be very ingenious indeed when the reward for cost-cutting is higher profit. Also, follow-on procurement of contracts would be based on performance by contractors who had found ways to cut costs instead of blowing them sky-high.

The Fitzgerald Case—Punishing the Thrifty

The present incentive to increase costs is at the heart of virtually every overrun. One of the most famous was the contract for the giant cargo plane C5A, upon which hangs the infamous tale of what happened to Ernest Fitzgerald.

Back in 1968 I summoned a brilliant young weapons expert from the air force to come before the Congressional Joint Economic Committee which I chaired. I asked him to confirm or deny a report I had heard that there was a very large overrun in the production of the plane. He hesitated to give figures. I suggested the overrun could have been as high as $2 billion (the highest for any weapons system on record at that time). He said he couldn't deny it.

That witness was Ernest Fitzgerald. The year before he refused to lie before my committee he had been given the highest decoration available for a civilian in the Defense Department for his brilliance in analyzing weapons systems. Because of his integrity he was put through one of the longest and cruelest ordeals in the history of the Pentagon.

The testimony he gave in 1968 was the end of his effective career in the air force. How he was disciplined is a telling example of the amazing persistence and power of the defense-contracting juggernaut.

In the first place, Fitzgerald turned out to be 100 percent right. There *was* a huge overrun on the C5A, exactly $2 billion, as Fitzgerald had concluded. That was bad news for Lockheed, who of course wanted to sell the plane to the Defense Department and for the Defense Department that wanted to buy it.

The ensuing plot to get rid of Fitzgerald began simply—just give him nothing significant to do. The best weapons analyst in the Pentagon was taken off weapons analysis. He was assigned, believe it or not, to the analysis of a twenty-lane bowling alley in Thailand. In justification, all they could come up with was that Fitzgerald was something of a skinflint—very careful about the way he spent his money!

Almost anyone else would have quit. Fitzgerald sued to get his job back—the job that he had handled so brilliantly that he had been cited for it with the highest honor possible. The suit took years. It cost hundreds of thousands of dollars. Thanks to fund raising and the help of the American Civil Liberties Union, Fitzgerald was able to persist. And he eventually won: this lone whistle blower took on four Presidents, the whole Pentagon, as well as the Civil Service, and he clobbered them in the courts. But they still wouldn't comply and they *still haven't.*

Fitzgerald first fell from grace by telling the truth during the Johnson Administration, which ended in 1969. When a Republican regime moved in, Fitzgerald had high hopes that a new party would let bygones be bygones and soon he would be back at work doing the job he knew better than anyone else. By no means. The Pentagon under Republican Nixon was no different from the Pentagon under Democrat Johnson. And with the accession of President Ford, Fitzgerald was still out in the cold.

The 1976 presidential campaign seemed to promise better things. Jimmy Carter actually made Fitzgerald an issue, among his other promises. He named Fitzgerald as a prime example of a man who had the courage to call attention to waste and incompetence in the federal government. Elect me, he was saying, and the Fitzgeralds of this world will be rewarded, not isolated and demeaned. Carter made it. New day for Fitzgerald? Forget it. For in spite of campaign vows that the new administration was going to reward truth and courage in its civil servants rather than punish them, Fitzgerald is still in a nothing job. In spite of entreaties to the President by this senator and others, in spite of support from Republicans and Democrats in both House and Senate who recognized the outrageousness of Fitzgerald's treatment, and despite a steady, never-recognized barrage of support from such highly respected men of the press as Clark Mollenhoff and others, Fitzgerald is still assigned nothing important and given no genuine responsibility.

One can only conclude that the military-industrial powers that be have become impervious to public or congressional criticism. The truth is known, proved, and there is still opportunity to set right the wrong. But no one is willing to take the step toward justice.

We now can make a good guess as to why Fitzgerald was originally fired. Certain White House tapes have been released. Speaking to White House aide Charles Colson, President Nixon said:

> This guy was fired. I'd marked it in the news summary. That's how it happened. I said get rid of that son of a bitch. You know, 'cause he is, he's been doin' this two or three times. So Seamans, who isn't much of a sandbagger, uh, will get rid of him I understand, uh, claimed executive privilege because he knew that I had ordered it.

President Nixon has flatly denied that he was referring here to Fitzgerald. And Ron Ziegler, who was then his press secretary, said that President Nixon had mistaken Fitzgerald for another person and had not intended to direct that Fitzgerald be fired.

Three Billion Destined for the Bottom of the Ocean

Apart from the billions the Defense Department wastes by allowing itself to be exploited by contractors for the useful weapons it buys, it wastes even more by buying obsolete weapons that are no longer good defense. This is a historic military weakness. It was years before our defense thinkers would admit the battleship was through. The manned bomber has been overtaken by the unmanned missile, but it may be decades and many billions of greenbacks before the air force is persuaded of that fact. But the most stunning example of waste is the acquisition of big new aircraft carriers. There is something about an aircraft carrier no navy man can resist. Whenever you see movies about the navy, the old glamour girl, the aircraft carrier, is there. Romantic, stately, spectacular, it takes remarkable skill to operate and more than a little courage in the pilots who attend it. It is useful in conventional war scenarios and in "showing the flag."

But it costs a bundle and then some—more than $3 billion, and its cost is going up every month with the fabulous expense of its planes, its support fleet, and so forth. The new ones being proposed are to stand up to the Soviet Union in the event of a direct confrontation. We already have thirteen carriers. The Soviet Union has two small ones. No other nation has built any.

Would a carrier be of any value in a nuclear war with the USSR? No way. The Russians and this country too have the capacity to center on and knock out an incoming missile the size of an ordinary desk even if that missile comes on at 17,000 miles an hour at varying altitudes from outer space. The carrier is as big as three football fields end to end and travels only fifty miles an hour at full speed. It has one altitude: sea level. As Senator Stuart Symington, who was a former Secretary of the Air Force, used to say, "It's like hitting a bull in the butt with a bull fiddle."

There goes your $3 billion to the bottom of the ocean, about five minutes after a "confrontation" begins.

(5)

The Many Facets of Waste

ONE DOESN'T HAVE to be in the military to feather one's pocket with government money. Here is the story of one official who lived the life of Riley on agency fleecing.

The Federal Deposit Insurance Corporation (FDIC), like a few other federal agencies, is supported not by your taxes, but by the levy it is permitted by Congress to impose on the nation's banks. For that reason it is exempt from the usual appropriation process, although we do try to follow how the funds are spent and we require a measure of accountability.

The chairman of the FDIC is, of course, a government official, and operates with funds that Congress, in effect, makes available through giving the FDIC the power to impose and collect this levy. Here is how former chairman Robert E. Barnett used those funds, according to a General Accounting Office report:

- The use of agency funds to pay the travel expenses of his wife, who accompanied him on seven trips to such exotic places as Puerto Rico (twice), Manila, and Mexico City. The FDIC was billed over $6100 to pay for these trips.
- Agency vehicles were used to transport Mrs. Barnett to the doctor and to take her and her children to the Hirschhorn Museum. The Barnett children were also in one instance chauffered to Rehoboth Beach by two FDIC employees using an agency car.
- The FDIC spent $1387.95 in June and July of 1976 to install locks and other security devices in Mr. Barnett's private residence.

- Two FDIC employees delivered surplus carpeting to the same residence. Mr. Barnett paid $.50 a yard.
- Upon leaving the agency, Mr. Barnett took two end tables from the agency's executive dining room, which he returned after being questioned by GAO investigators.
- The FDIC paid Mr. Barnett's membership fees in a private club in Virginia.

It seems to me outrageous that the head of a federal agency can use its funds for his personal benefit. Even though these funds are derived from fees and premiums assessed against commercial banks, the cost is ultimately passed on to the public in the form of higher prices for bank services. I see no reason why we should have one ethical standard for the bank regulatory agencies and a stricter standard for the rest of the government officials.

Such items as this one, and there are many, might be dismissed as petty chiseling. But they mount up, and taken as a whole I think they indicate the need for closer budgetary and accounting controls over agencies that are immune to annual audits by the GAO.

The Limousines

Have you ever been to Washington and seen the limousines wheeling along the avenues with liveried chauffeurs? There is usually just one man in the back seat of each of them; a light is on and he may be reading—maybe reports, the racing form, or the funnies. You may think, Ha, I've spotted the Secretary of State. Or the Vice President. Or even the President himself. Unfortunately, you are kidding yourself. What you are seeing is usually some down-the-line official you've never heard of. There are literally hundreds of them going to and fro in government limousines.

You and I are paying for this. First, for the chauffeur and the car. The fleet of limousines chauffering officials to work and home again in Washington alone is estimated to cost almost $5 million. Second, the chauffered bureaucrat pays no income tax on this fringe luxury—which gouges the Treasury as much as $2.5 million.

Under the law, Title 31, Section 638a, government cars may be used only for "official purposes," which do *not* include being driven to work. The only exceptions are the President, specific cabinet officers, ambassadors, doctors on duty to see patients, and government employees on field service.

White House staff, generals and admirals, undersecretaries, assistant secretaries, heads of agencies like the Veterans' Administration, NASA, EPA, FEA, the SEC, and so on, are specifically not eligible for that free service under this law.

Nevertheless, about 175 officials in Washington and many more outside Washington are driven to and from work, all but a handful of them in violation of the law.

In hearings I have held as Chairman of the Subcommittee on HUD-Independent Agencies of the Senate Appropriations Committee, it was revealed that maintenance and depreciation and fuel costs of a limousine come to about $2800 each a year. The chauffeur cost averages $25,000 a year. In most cases two drivers are required, and they earn large amounts of overtime.

On September 5, 1975, the Treasury Department printed in the *Federal Register* a "Discussion Draft of Regulations" on "fringe benefits" that would be treated as gross income and subject to taxation. Example II clearly states that officials not exempted under Title 31, Section 638a, would be taxed for the fair market value of the chauffeur and limousine service when the regulations went into effect.

But they are still not in effect five years later!

Meanwhile the Treasury and IRS have cracked down on such groups as insurance salesmen who are provided cars for use in their business. They are not only being taxed currently for the "imputed income" based on the value of using company cars to go to and from home, but the IRS has called them in, reviewed their old tax returns, and taxed them for previous years as well.

Why should government officials go scot free? As most high-ranking government employees are in the 50 percent marginal income tax bracket, the tax could amount to as much as $14,000 per big shot receiving the full, chauffered, portal-to-portal service. Using the modest number of 175 individuals taking this benefit (and not counting those in regional offices, military installations, and embassies abroad), the government is losing almost $2.5 million a year in taxes.

What's more, if these taxes were collected, most limousiners would kick the habit, and there would be a further savings of at least $4.9 million.

*

According to its own Public Affairs Office newsletter, the Federal Aviation Administration (FAA) spent over $417,000 to keep weather forecasters from getting wet. I really can't improve on their own description of the new luxury:

> RAINDROPS WON'T BE FALLING ON YOUR HEADS . . .
> A $361,150 [later increased to $417,150] contract for 79 [later increased to 95] Remote Readout Hygrothermometers will permit FAA personnel making weather observations to tell if it's likely to rain without running the risk of getting caught in it. The hygrothermometers measure the likelihood of rain by comparing the temperature within a bulb of completely dry air with the temperature of the moisture-laden air around it. When the two temperatures get within three degrees, rain is likely. *Existing hygrothermometers do this now* [italics mine], but the FAA employees have to go outside to read them. The new ones, which will be made by the Airflo Instrument Company of Glastonbury, Conn., will relay the temperature to inside monitors where they can be read in indoor comfort.

The FAA, I should note, now contends that these new instruments are needed "in the interest of better observations and more efficient manpower utilization." This attempt at justification came after my inquiry about the hygrothermometer contract—a quickie rationale for what is, in fact, an inexcusable indulgence that leaves the American taxpayer "out in the rain."

*

Another fiscal item that to my mind can only be called a boon-doggle is the month-long, free summer vacation donated to chosen doctors, lawyers, and school administrators at the middling stage of their careers who must easily be earning more than $30,000 a year. To them that hath shall be given. The National Endowment for the Humanities evidently decided that the many years of undergraduate and graduate education these professionals undergo is inadequate, and that a seminar for "concentrated midcareer humanistic study" at Uncle Sam's expense is just the remedy needed. These tuition-free sessions at some of the most delectable university watering holes are intended "to broaden and sharpen their humanistic perspectives."

The National Endowment is an $82-million-a-year agency. Federal spending for the humanities has nearly doubled in the past two years. It started with five of these seminars in the fiscal year 1974. By 1976 they had increased the number fourfold to twenty. The taxpayer paid about $3000 for each of the well-heeled participants. Not only were their transportation and textbooks covered, but each beneficiary received a stipend of $1200. The locations of the seminars ranged from Stanford at the foot of San Francisco Bay to Williams College in the Berkshires. All were held in the summer. The discussions which, according to the brochure, "can help to clarify understanding of the fundamental issues facing modern society" were limited to about three hours a day.

It should be stressed again that those attending the seminars were not struggling scholars or researchers, but professionals well into the upper-middle-income bracket. A $12,000-a-year factory worker who pays a $2000 income tax might well wonder why these professionals cannot afford their own transportation and must have a stipend to raise their humanistic consciousness.

*

On the same wave length, the Office of Education paid out $40,375 to give bored bureaucrats a new lease on life, with "creative career and life planning" courses during working hours. The cost for each participant was $1100 and, oddly enough, the same course with the same instructors could have been taken on an employee's own time for $475.

Some of the things the students were taught during the ten days of three and a half hour sessions were:

1. to take a holistic rather than an atomistic approach to life;
2. to write a 50- to 200-page autobiography;
3. to analyze their hobbies;
4. to keep their eyes on the "divine radar";
5. to figure out, in Walter Mitty fashion, how they would give away $10 million;
6. to reconstruct a written diary of their entire lives in which they "boast a lot";
7. to conduct an on-site personal survey of a community in the general area in which they live, talking to people according to a well-thought-out plan that leaves room for "improvisation, serendipity, and the chance encounter."

My argument is not against the private firm which gave the course, the talented authors of the official textbook, nor the employees who want to take the course—if they pay for it out of their own pockets. My objection is to the government picking up the tab.

The officials in the Office of Education announced the course as helping employees "determine their goals in life and make changes in their environment, lifestyle, careers, and direction which will aid them in gaining satisfaction both on the job and in their personal life."

After this display of questionable allocation of public funds, they may wish to consider seriously the issue of changing careers themselves, or, as the textbooks put it, to do a "functional analysis" of their "transferable skills."

*

The Department of Labor in 1977 granted a $384,948 contract to hire 101 persons, under the Comprehensive Employment and Training Act (CETA) to do a door-to-door survey of the number of dogs, cats, and horses in or around 160,000 houses and apartments in Ventura County, California.

Doesn't that sound like the old WPA make-work syndrome? That agency was criticized for its "leaf-raking" projects, but during the Great Depression, with as much as 25 percent of our work force unemployed, there was justification for a good number of its programs. In 1977 we had a pretty vigorous economic recovery, adding millions of permanent, private-sector jobs to the rolls. Conditions were very different from those in 1934. And while the Constitution requires a decennial census of the people living in the U.S.A., spending taxpayers' money to count the animals should cause the Founding Fathers to turn in their graves.

CETA funds are supposed not only to provide jobs but also to satisfy some unmet, pressing local need. According to the proposal submitted to the Department of Labor, they needed to find out how many dogs were not immunized against rabies. This sounds good (with horses and cats thrown in to make a longer survey), but as a fact, the Animal Regulation Department of Ventura County admitted to my staff that there had not been a case of rabies among dogs or cats or horses in the county for more than a decade. The real carriers of rabies are not the domestic but certain wild animals anyway.

I only hope the Department of Labor does not contemplate financing attempts to count bats, rats, squirrels, and skunks. They may be held back by the flak they got in Ventura

County from both private citizens and federal officials.

In spite of all the criticism, local officials doggedly persisted in a useless make-work program, maintaining that local revenue would be raised through the sale of licenses to owners of unregistered dogs. If this were a cost-effective method of raising funds, county dog catchers would have started pounding on all the doors in America. Obviously the survey gouged out a slice of federal tax dollars in order to raise relatively few dollars for a local government. Robbing Peter to pay Paul is a perfect example of what can happen when the unit of government that spends the money is not the same as the one that has to raise it in the first place.

Why didn't the Department of Labor put its foot down? Their excuse is that under CETA the state and local prime sponsors have the authority and responsibility vis-à-vis the priorities of local projects. According to the Labor Department, as long as the amount of money spent does not exceed the allocation of funds to a certain area, it cannot, or at least will not, second-guess local officials.

In this case, the result of that policy was a mindless, irrelevant waste of federal resources that might have been spent for something the community actually needed.

*

Another California county threw federal money down the drain with a CETA project to survey the number of Samoans living in its midst. And for the final touch of absurdity, even those making the survey didn't care enough about it to hold on to the figures; they just plain lost them.

The Department of Labor funded a $140,000, uncompleted census of the Samoan population in Orange County, California. It was contracted, under the CETA Public Service Jobs Program, to a nonprofit corporation called the Institute of Emergent Nationalisms Determinacy, Inc., largely created and definitely controlled by the members of a single family. The corporation came into being only a few months before it received the CETA grant. Four months after a final report was due, even the limited raw data allegedly collected was not found, and the former head of the program is reported to be in Western Samoa, outside U.S. jurisdiction. Attempts to contact him have so far failed.

Labor Department spokesmen justified their lack of oversight of the grant on grounds that it was locally reviewed and controlled. And one local official said, according to the Orange County *Register,* that he is not upset by the lack of any finished product to show for the money.

> The purpose of the contract was to provide employment and training to unemployed Santa Ana residents and a by-product of this was to be a study. Just because the study wasn't completed I don't think it can be said the city got the raw end of things. That's the philosophy of the CETA program.

Who gets "the raw end of things" is something I must have made pretty clear by now.

There are enough useful and constructive projects—including genuine help to Samoans in need—to offer to those who are unemployed and willing to work without resorting to ridiculous, unmotivated make-work. Congress should reexamine the procedures that have led to this lack of common sense.

Useless Paperwork

Possibly more common than the funding of studies that serve no purpose is the even more exasperating waste of public money to produce the elaborate specifications that are so time-consuming they blow the cost of procurement out of sight. Here's a classic.

The Bureau of Land Management required useless paperwork which sent the contract almost four times too high. One hundred fifty-five pages of requirements, including twenty-three fold-out diagrams, were sent to forty-one companies for bids on fire equipment to be placed on two pickup trucks. Only two companies responded with a bid. The lower estimate won at a level of $15,497 per unit—not including the trucks.

Why such a poor response, and why such a high bid? Because of the paperwork. According to one firm, Fire-x Corporation, the fire equipment could have been supplied for $4000 per unit without the complicated and extensive government requirements detailing the placement of every screw and bolt. In order to bid at all, a firm would have had to charge three to five times more than for a commercial order, so they could hire ten extra employees for pushing paper alone.

It has been estimated that the total cost to the federal government and private business for filling out official forms runs as high as $36 billion annually. Over 130 million man-hours a year are lost on paper shuffling. Unfortunately this is increasing each year—by 50 percent since 1967, according to one report. It seems to be an epidemic spreading through the government.

In order to cut down on wasteful and unnecessary paperwork, I have introduced a Form Reform Bill. This would make every government form obsolete after five years. Before any new or old form could be used, it would have to be simplified and certified by the Comptroller General.

Research Waste

Time and time again, I have locked horns in committee with the top men in the National Science Foundation and NASA over the value of mammoth research spending to the economy, to the Gross National Product (GNP), and to the general good of our citizens. I have had the same locking of horns with senators over the mammoth amounts shoveled out for research in the Defense Department.

This does not mean I am against scientific research; it is obviously vitally necessary. My theme is *proportion, moderation, common sense.*

The argument that we can't maintain our world leadership

Output per Hour in Manufacturing, Eleven Countries, 1950–1977
(Average Annual Percentage Change)

Year[1]	United States	Canada	Japan	Belgium	Denmark	France	Germany	Italy	Netherlands	Sweden	United Kingdom
1950–51	3.3	4.1	24.8	0.0	1.2	5.2	3.0	11.7	3.6	2.9	0.0
1951–52	1.8	2.7	5.3	0.0	-0.9	3.3	9.5	4.0	2.4	-0.3	-4.1
1952–53	1.8	3.5	13.7	0.0	1.4	5.2	7.1	5.0	7.9	5.5	4.7
1953–54	1.4	4.4	7.1	0.0	4.3	3.0	4.1	5.3	3.8	-0.1	3.4
1954–55	5.0	6.5	5.0	0.0	2.6	4.9	6.4	8.9	5.2	1.3	3.2
1955–56	-0.8	4.2	6.6	0.0	2.8	6.5	2.6	5.5	6.0	6.1	0.1
1956–57	2.1	0.7	9.1	0.0	3.7	1.6	8.8	1.9	3.9	5.2	2.4
1957–58	-0.5	3.4	-6.6	0.0	3.5	3.9	5.0	1.7	2.3	4.6	1.7
1958–59	4.4	5.4	16.5	0.0	6.8	7.3	8.1	7.6	7.3	6.1	4.1
1959–60	1.2	3.5	15.2	0.0	3.3	5.2	7.0	6.3	5.2	3.3	5.9
1960–61	2.4	5.4	12.9	1.7	5.6	4.6	5.4	8.1	5.4	4.7	0.8
1961–62	4.6	5.2	4.4	7.0	5.2	4.6	6.2	10.8	3.1	7.4	2.5
1962–63	7.0	3.8	8.3	3.5	3.2	5.9	4.6	2.7	2.9	5.8	5.4
1963–64	5.3	4.4	13.2	6.1	8.2	5.1	7.4	5.9	9.5	9.1	7.2
1964–65	3.2	3.8	4.2	4.7	5.0	5.7	6.5	11.2	6.3	8.0	3.1
1965–66	1.6	3.4	10.0	7.0	5.0	7.0	3.5	6.0	6.6	4.1	3.6
1966–67	0.2	3.2	14.8	6.7	9.8	5.6	6.5	5.9	6.9	8.5	4.4
1967–68	3.7	6.8	12.6	9.2	9.8	11.4	6.9	7.9	12.2	10.1	7.1
1968–69	1.1	5.9	15.5	8.8	9.6	3.7	6.0	7.6	9.3	7.4	1.2
1969–70	-0.4	1.5	12.7	9.0	7.4	5.0	2.4	4.8	9.3	5.3	0.2
1970–71	5.4	7.1	3.1	5.7	7.3	5.3	4.6	2.9	6.8	3.6	4.0
1971–72	5.1	4.6	7.5	12.0	8.6	5.8	6.0	8.1	7.9	6.9	7.3
1972–73	2.7	4.5	11.7	10.1	6.0	5.5	6.2	12.1	10.2	6.9	4.1
1973–74	-5.2	1.7	0.3	6.2	3.3	2.8	6.1	5.3	8.3	3.1	1.1
1974–75	4.9	-2.4	-3.9	5.2	7.8	2.7	3.8	-4.3	-2.1	-1.1	-2.7
1975–76	4.3	4.6	8.1	9.5	7.5	9.1	8.2	8.4	10.6	1.6	3.4
1976–77	2.3	4.8	5.6	3.3	2.4	5.2	4.2	0.9	3.6	2.4	-1.6

[1]Preliminary estimates for latest year.

Note: The data relate to all employed persons (wage and salary earners, the self-employed, and unpaid family workers) in the United States and Canada, and all employees (wage and salary earners) in the other countries.

Prepared by U.S. Department of Labor, Bureau of Labor Statistics, Office of Productivity and Technology, November 29, 1978.

and improve productivity without colossal investment in basic research overlooks the fact that the results of basic research are an international commodity; they are there for the taking by any nation with the technological sophistication to apply them.

How else explain that productivity growth in Germany and Japan has year after year outstripped our own, despite the fact that we support more than 50 percent of the basic research and development performed in the world? We spend more on it per capita, more as a percentage of the GNP, far more in actual *amount* than the more productive nations. Equivalently, we have more scientists and engineers per 10,000 of the population in the labor force.

The figures speak for themselves, as shown by the two tables included here.

Research and Development (R&D) Expenditures as a Percentage of GNP

Year	United States	France	Germany	Japan	United Kingdom
1961	2.74	1.38	N.A.	1.39	2.39
1962	2.73	1.46	1.25	1.47	N.A.
1963	2.89	1.55	1.41	1.44	N.A.
1964	2.97	1.81	1.57	1.48	2.30
1965	2.91	2.01	1.73	1.54	N.A.
1966	2.90	2.03	1.81	1.48	2.32
1967	2.91	2.13	1.97	1.53	2.33
1968	2.83	2.08	1.97	1.61	2.29
1969	2.74	1.97	2.05	1.65	2.23
1970	2.64	1.85	2.18	1.79	N.A.
1971	2.50	1.86	2.38	1.84	N.A.
1972	2.43	1.81	2.33	1.85	2.06
1973	2.34	1.73	2.22	1.89	N.A.
1974	2.32	1.74	2.26	1.95	N.A.
1975	2.30	1.82	2.39	1.94	2.05
1976	2.27	1.74	2.28	1.94	N.A.
1977	2.25	N.A.	2.26	N.A.	N.A.

N.A. = not available.
Source: National Science Foundation.
Prepared by U.S. Department of Labor, Office of Productivity and Technology, Division of Foreign Labor Statistics and Trade, January 1979.

The constant cry for more research dollars has become a reflex action for members of the executive and legislative branches alike. This is of course partially in response to heavy lobbying pressure from the academic community; universities often use research money to offset declining enrollments and inflationary costs.

The Experts

What do the scientific experts say? Here's an excerpt from a report on federal Research and Development (R & D) funding put out by the distinguished American Association for the Advancement of Science.

> The simplistic view is that R & D helps the economy through a sequence of events something like this: you start with basic research and move on through applied research, development, technological innovation, increased productivity, and economic growth, and finally get a general advance in economic welfare.
>
> Of course, it's not that simple. . . . *All* basic research does not (and should not be expected to) lead to applied research, development, innovation, and ultimately to an advance in economic welfare. It is true that *no* basic research by itself causes an increase in economic welfare. It takes many other actions, and the external conditions have to be right, for this to happen.

Perhaps the most controversial views on federal support for basic research come from a California professor, Dr. Allen Rosenstein, who teaches engineering at UCLA. This thesis was summed up in the *Houston Chronicle.*

> American policy makers and educators must realize, said Rosenstein, that while basic scientific research or knowledge for knowledge's sake may win prestige and awards, it is the expertise of the public-oriented professions that determines a nation's economic and environmental standards.
>
> "The dichotomy," said Rosenstein, "is well understood in Japan

and on the European continent, but has been ignored in the English-speaking countries."

Seeking "academic respectability" through pure scholarship, and encouraged by the influence of the prestigious National Science Foundation, professional schools gradually transformed their faculty makeup and curriculum.

One result of the shift, says Rosenstein, has been that while Japan and the non-English-speaking countries of Western Europe are turning out true professionals and rapidly increasing their productivity, the English-speaking countries—Britain, the United States and Canada—have lagged far behind in productivity.

Thus, while academic folklore insists that more resources committed to basic research the better, Rosenstein points to the lack of correlation between a nation's basic research ability and its ability in the marketplace.

What's the answer? Certainly we should not eliminate all federal support for basic research. But neither should we expect big increases in funding for it to boost our national productivity. We should husband with wisdom our scarce resources and make sure we spend the *appropriate* amount of tax dollars for the right kind of basic research, emphasizing quality rather than quantity.

We should also do our best to make sure that our scientific breakthroughs and know-how are not isolated in federally supported ivory towers of academe. Moreover, it should be remembered that *over*spending for basic research not only contributes to the national budget deficit, but it also puts the federal government in competition with private industry for scientists and their invaluable contributions.

Promotional Waste

A most unusual extravaganza can occur when a government agency forgets what it is and decides to adopt objectives and tactics of a typical private firm.

When a businessman wants to make more money he has to

increase his volume. He advertises, promotes, and hires high-priced salesmen. His extra sales increase profits as long as unit costs don't rise, and usually costs actually drop because the larger volume does not require proportionately increased over-head.

That's fine and solid common sense in the world of trade. But it doesn't apply in the public sector. The U.S. Postal Service made a real boner trying to ape smart businessmen.

They spent over $3.4 million on a Madison Avenue ad campaign to get Americans to write more letters to each other. Then, compounding their folly, they spent almost $775,000 more in a seemingly futile effort to test whether their campaign was working—a classic case of throwing good money after bad. It tallied up to a grand total of $4 million.

A government agency should not get into the game of drumming up business for itself. God forbid the Defense Department should start a war in order to use military hardware more efficiently. (Or to acquire more.) We do not ask Social Security contributors to retire earlier so we can make more efficient use of the computers that send out the checks.

To be fair, let's look first at the theoretically good intentions of the Postal Service when it launched its Household Correspondence Program. They claimed that a greater volume of first-class mail would produce more revenues. As one of the senior officials wrote me:

> Personal letter writing volume has not grown in recent years and moreover, total first class mail is expected to decline in future years as a result of increased reliance upon electric transfers. Since first class mail is the major revenue producer for the Postal Service and manpower and equipment are presently available to handle additional volume, increased household correspondence would provide additional revenues.

In the face of staggering deficits the agency came up with a multimillion-dollar ad campaign, and now can't seem to figure out how to test its results, which is why they say they may spend another million to see if it has done any good.

Propaganda to try to make Americans more prolific letter writers is a dubious project at best. People write letters for many reasons, but I doubt that a public relations pitch from the government is one of them. This venture belongs on the junkpile, along with other ill-conceived schemes such as unjustified rate increases and the proposal to end Saturday deliveries.

There are lots of other possibilities for the Postal Service to ponder if it wants to increase revenues. As one of their Madison Avenue friends might put it, it's time for them to run these options up the flagpole and see if anyone salutes.

In the meantime, the burden of their bad judgment and impetuous spending is something our taxpayers should not be asked to bear and our treasury cannot afford.

(6)

The Public Works Rip-off

THERE IS ONE all-too-human, prevalent weakness of members of Congress that costs you literally billions every year—the weakness for public works. For many representatives and senators, visualizing the coming campaign for reelection and the opponent who asks that perennial question of his home state audience, "What's your congressman ever done for you?" there is just one answer—the public works project teased out of the federal budget for that home state or district.

It's the perfect answer. "What do you mean I haven't done anything for you? Look at that dam I got you." It's perfect because it's specific, concrete, irrefutable. Maybe it's a new public building or a park. Not a generality like the consumer protection bill or an improved housing finance law. A public works project you can see; hundreds of voters got employment out of it; property values increased. It may have cost the nation far more than it's worth, but the people in that congressional district have come out ahead, and the overwhelming majority in the rest of the country haven't even heard about it.

And ah, the crowning glory. A member of Congress may even have that shiny building or elaborate multimillion-dollar park named after *him*. Wow, immortality! "Maybe my grandchild, or my great-grandchild will say the senator must have been quite a guy—a big fat park named after him."

The result? Tens of billions spent on public works that have cost 50, maybe 100, percent more than they should have.

Many of these projects may be well worth while. This is a stronger country economically because we have a highway system that is the envy of the rest of the world. A good number of our inland waterways, flood control systems, and irrigation aids have brought more benefits to the nation than they cost.

But on the whole these benefits go to a relatively few persons, that is, those who work on a public project, those whose homes will be protected from flood, and those particular farmers whose fields will be irrigated. And an infinite variety of such public projects is going to be proposed by a self-speaking, determined band of promoters.

To provide some discipline and moderation, the government has developed a rare system of requiring that promoters demonstrate that the benefits of a project will exceed its cost—a type of "scientific selection." If this great idea were fully and consistently carried out, we would save an astronomical amount every year. The tax burden would be lower, so would inflation, and probably half of our recent public works projects would never have been built. Nor would half of those now on the consideration list go through.

The difficulty is that both the benefits and costs are computed by a government agency called the Corps of Engineers, who operate under the strong pressure, guidance, and fiscal control of the Public Works Committees of the House and Senate. These committees are manned and chaired by members of Congress who generally believe strongly that public works are a great thing for the country and especially for their own states. Each legislator importunes and is in turn importuned by colleagues to approve a project in "my" state or "my" district. As the backscratching goes on, they put together a bill that becomes a legislative juggernaut. Senator Paul Douglas some years ago vigorously protested just such an elephantine bill. The chairman of the committee, Senator Dennis Chavez, couldn't understand Douglas's objection. "After all," he declared, "there's something in this bill for everybody."

Must we grow bananas on Pikes Peak? Theoretically, with enough water and solar reflection, we could do it. But how about the benefit-cost ratio? Wouldn't that protect the taxpayer from such a wild notion? The answer is a resounding *no*.

To be sure, the West is arid, and for some senators, from that part of the country especially, public works are a way of life. A federal water project can make arid land fertile; it can increase the value of what was marginal or even wasteland. So the pressure to justify a water project is heavy. In some cases it is completely reasonable; in others the funding is absurd.

The Corps of Engineers, under pressure from Congress, has become expert in inventing benefits. The fertility a project will immediately bring can be estimated overoptimistically, as can the value of the crop that will rise up ten, twelve, or twenty years from now. Recreation benefits can be added. Often a water project involves a man-made lake for fishing, boating, swimming, and a big potential increase in property values all around the shore. But that's just the beginning.

The benefits—against which the Appropriations Committee must weigh the cost—won't be enjoyed until the public work is used up, which may take up to fifty years. (In the past, the life of some projects has been estimated to have been a hundred years.)

That's where the sleight-of-hand, tricky calculus comes in. To estimate the value of a project twenty-five or fifty years from now, you have to discount (that is, reduce) it over time. The "value" will depend on the way you do it.

The benefits are reduced because you don't receive them for many years; the longer a project takes to build, the more the value to the public goes down. This reduction, or discount, depends on two things: the number of years you have to wait and —this is the tricky one—on the percentage rate at which you discount the future benefit during those years before it is realized.

To understand the immense difference the "discount factor"

makes, consider that, at a 6 percent discount factor, a million dollars you or your heirs receive fifty years from now is worth $54,288 today, but at 12 percent that million dollars fifty years from now is worth only $3460 today. Do you see why the public works boys battle for the low discount factor? It justifies public works that just aren't worth it.

The Corps of Engineers has been able to minimize, on paper, the reduction of the benefit value of a project after twenty to fifty years by foisting a pitifully unrealistic 6 percent discount factor on their projects, although the long-term opportunity cost of money is at 12 percent. Twelve percent is what the typical return has been throughout the years in the private sector before taxes, and that's the fair comparison. By reducing the future loss of value and putting the costs all up front, they create the illusion that the benefits will exceed the costs, and they get the go-ahead from Congress.

Public works roll on because members of Congress who make the decisions want them for their own districts or states. The Corps of Engineers accommodates their wishes by vastly exaggerating the benefits of the projects through this systematic use of a grossly unjustified discount factor and by a happy optimism about recreational and property value advantages.

Then there are the cost overruns. Compared to the Corps of Engineers, we have marvels of efficiency in the Defense Department, HEW, and GSA. The Corps deserves the title of Overrun King if only because so many of their projects break the 100 percent overrun mark.

Of 178 recent construction projects, 83 of them, or 47 percent, went over by 100 percent or more, topping the record without any doubt for the most costly mismanagement in the entire government. The baseline cost of these 178 projects was first estimated at $12.7 billion. Congress authorized them and began funding. Now the same bunch will cost $26.7 billion, because of overruns.

Such projects are concentrated heavily in the South and West.

Under the Corps's flood control program, the following dramatic increases stand out: Caesar Creek, Ohio, up 243 percent; Cooper Lake, Texas, up 325 percent; Fire Island Inlet, New York, up 325 percent; New Orleans to Venice Hurricane Protection, up 1027 percent; Sacramento River Bank, up 356 percent. Among its navigation projects, Jacksonville Harbor, Florida, is up 316 percent, and the Tennessee-Tombigbee Waterway, Alabama, up 321 percent.

These dramatic cost overruns cannot be explained away by inflation. When the General Accounting Office analyzed them, it found that at least half the increase was for changes in engineering, in estimating, and in the scope of the project. These changes could have been avoided, given thorough and proper planning.

The Corps provides critical service to the country. The number of lives lost and the amount of property destroyed would be immeasurably greater if it were not for their protection.

But along with that protection have come environmental disasters as well: the loss of anadromous fish spawning grounds, destruction of wildlife habitats, channelization of streambeds, silting and death of lakes, and countless other problems. It seems to be a good time for the Executive Department to rethink the function of the Corps of Engineers. Perhaps they should be directed to reclaiming polluted waterways and building municipal waste treatment facilities and other desperately needed capital programs where their engineering resources could be efficiently used.

Congress's Public Works Darlings

When the Senate and the House venture into their own private public works they have a propensity to be incredibly inefficient. The new Senate Office Building, now known as the Dirksen Building, and the Rayburn Building—put up in the sixties—are examples of a spirit of gay abandon when it comes to tossing federal money to the skies. A more recent showplace is the Hart addition to the new Senate Office Building, known familiarly and properly in Washington as the new S.O.B.

The construction of both these buildings was waste at its worst. In the Dirksen Building, the metal hands of the clocks were so elaborate, expensive, and heavy that they couldn't move. The floors in the offices were covered with the best and brightest linoleum that money could buy. But it was decided to cover the fancy linoleum with luxurious carpeting on the lame excuse that the lineoleum might be too slippery for Senate secretaries and they couldn't risk having fallen women in the offices. But then, after the carpeting was firmly in place, it was found that the beautiful, expensive doors wouldn't close over the new carpets. So the doors had to be taken off and planed down.

Every Senate office was equipped with a safe so elaborate it would do justice to Tiffany's or a bank. Senators do not harbor classified material, so the safes were put to use to guard the most precious of all jewels: the senators' liquor supplies.

But the Dirksen Building was only the beginning. At four times the cost of the original building ($125 to $200 million) the Senate constructed an addition that would make a Persian prince green with envy. It includes such "national prestige" items as a rooftop dining room and a *third* gymnasium. These luxury items show an arrogance that should turn taxpayers livid. We already had two dining rooms. We already had a gym in the Russell Building and a rarely used one in the Dirksen Building. The third "physical fitness center" has a convertible basketball/handball/tennis court. The average American, whose dollars pay for this indulgence, has no access to such facilities. If senators want to stay in shape, why shouldn't they pay for membership in a health club?

The landscaping and art work around the building and the proliferation of marble and bronze throughout the building are excessive to the point of a late Roman atmosphere. The senators' offices are wood paneled, of course—$1.5 million for this alone.

The final cost was two and one-half to five times the original estimate, or a cost overrun of 154 percent to 300 percent. Like Topsy, it just growed and growed. And it hasn't stopped yet.

In 1972, just to get a foot in the door, this new office building was proposed to the Senate, at a cost of $47,925,000. Later the scope of the building was broadened considerably, requiring an additional appropriation of $20.9 million. Since then, appropriations have risen to an astronomical $141 million—with another $100 million pending.

The reasons for the king-sized overruns are several: built-in incentives to spend, delays coupled with rising costs, and the addition of aforesaid unnecessary luxury features.

What were the incentives for the contractors to spend as much as possible? The contracts awarded by the Senate stipulated a flat 6 percent fee for the whole project. This means no penalties for cost increases; the fees would be $3 million if the building cost $50 million. But as the building has increased in cost to over $100 million, the fees have gone up past $6 million. Such a flat-fee contract means that the more changes or goldplating the Senate or the architect of the Capitol comes up with, the more everybody cleans up.

With inflation running high, each month's delay costs hundreds of thousands. And there have been many months of delay. Completion was originally forecast for May 1977, later set for January 1978, and at that point jumped to June 1981. An inordinate amount of time has been taken on preparation of drawings and specifications, on the review of same, and on letting bids and contracts. As a result, a big hole, half a city block long, sat waiting for the superstructure for ten costly months.

Ironically, the building is named for the late Senator Philip A. Hart—the most averse to pomp or show of all senators!

In all fairness, the architect does deserve credit for increasing the amount of usable office space and for instituting an energy-saving design.

But one cannot fail to make the interesting comparison between the record of the Hart Building and that of the new Air and Space Museum on the Mall, which was completed before its deadline, had no cost overrun, yet included four additional major features within the original cost estimate.

Building outrageously ornate buildings is only one of the areas where Congress takes care of itself.

First, the Senate recently approved the addition of up to three new committee staff employees per senator at a salary of $33,975 each. While some senators may think twice before using their full allotment and adding $102,000 to their budget, it is estimated that about half will do so, at a total cost of around $5 million to the taxpayer.

This appropriation, incredible as it was, was a watered-down version of the original proposal sponsored by 56 of 100 senators, which called for more than 1000 new employees at a cost of $40.9 million.

The idea that bigger staffs are necessary in order to cut spending by the Executive Branch is an illusion. Two of the most effective congressional budget cutters, John Williams of Delaware and H. R. Gross of Iowa, operated with small, efficient staffs. I have found, in my own experience of taking on the Supersonic Transport (SST), military waste, and bureaucratic rip-offs, that one or two members of my own or committee staffs are far more efficient than a congressional bureaucracy.

Unfortunately, the Senate, in enlarging its perquisites and prerogatives, took its cue from the House of Representatives. Early in 1975, the House Administration Committee, through a series of orders, increased the expense allowances for equipment, travel, newsletters, phones, and so forth, by $23,000 a member for a total of $10 million. The House then added some 735 new staff positions at an additional minimum cost of $6 million.

All this reinforced the push for more space and new buildings.

While the House turned it down the first year, the architect of the Capitol is pressing for a fourth House Office Building. The preliminary costs alone are $22.5 million. Because of the new staff increase, ultimate approval is inevitable. In view of the history of the Rayburn Building, the price tag will probably be $200 million—$50 million more than the Sears Building in Chicago, which, with its 110 stories and 4.5 million square feet, is both the tallest and largest private office building in the world.

The ultimate congressional folly was the $1.3 million the House decided to spend to automate nineteen elevators but retain operators to run them.

*

The story of the $100,000, 100-foot baseball bat is a dismaying one.

In a deeply depressed economy such as ours in the thirties, the Works Progress Administration kept art and artistic endeavor alive. But in a pluralist society, especially when it is prosperous, as much as possible should be left to the individual and the private foundation sponsorship of art. The heavy hand of government may be tasteful and discriminating or it may bring forth abominations, but if it is the heavy hand of government it comes from a single source of great power and can have a deadening effect on artistic standards.

The General Services Administration (GSA) spent $1,015,000 for fifteen statues, murals, or other "art" to decorate federal buildings under the Art in Architecture program. Which brings us to our gigantic red steel baseball bat. It's in a plaza of a federal building in Chicago and is called a "high structural latticed column in red painted steel." But if it's not a baseball bat, then I'm blind as a bat. A statue of Babe Ruth or Ernie Banks, the legendary Cubs star, would have been more appropriate. According to the statement of the GSA (I am not going to get into the ticklish subject of "what is art"), they are promoting works "intended to be an integral part of the total architectural design and enhance the building's environment for the occupants and the general public." How a 100-foot, red baseball bat becomes an integral part of the Federal Building is beyond me. In fact, I'd bet that many occupants of the building and many who are forced to pass by find it distracting and in bad taste.

Other questionable items are, in my opinion, a $34,000 mural in Wilmington, Delaware; a 54-foot high, red steel arch for that same Federal Building in Chicago; a sculpture for Las Cruces, New Mexico, which looks like the tail of a yellow whale sounding; a rusty piece of farm machinery in the guise of sculpture in St. Paul, Minnesota, which cost $42,500; five steel pilings for $45,000 in Rochester, New York; a life-sized representation of a restaurant scene for $60,000 in Buffalo.

Some projects have come off far better—for instance, the five pieces of carved granite in Seattle, though one wonders about the $100,000 price tag.

Modern art is usually experimental. But should the general public pay for fads that give them neither pleasure nor emotional lift? We are a nation of enormous talent and good judgment. The GSA should apply its own sensible standard as quoted above before spending another dime on public "art" that is still so controversial, if not upsetting, to the average Americans who are paying for it.

*

FEDERAL BUREAUCRATS MAKE WAVES AND THE TAXPAYER GETS SOAKED. This headline signaled a historic moment in American history and a fleece that got me in trouble with the mayor of Salt Lake City.

The Mormons are among the most prudent and economical of our citizens and Utah consistently sends to the Senate members who fight hard to hold down spending. But even they are vulnerable to the public works virus. That is why the Bureau of Outdoor Recreation of the Department of the Interior was bamboozled into spending $145,000 to install a wave-making machine in a specially designed, double-Olympic-sized swimming pool in Salt Lake City.

According to local officials, the 4-foot surf created by the machine "would provide a recreation experience not available in an inland society—an experience of the rushing water of a river or wave action you can only get at the ocean." (The white water of the Colorado River evidently doesn't count.) Based on this rationale, the public will be asked next to fund ski slopes in Florida, artificial mountains in Indiana, igloos made of imported snow in Death Valley, and tropical rain forests in Wisconsin.

The gigantic pool is only part of a larger complex including a marina, boat ramp, bath house, and parking lot. The cost of the entire thing is estimated at $1,008,000, $500,000 of which will be supplied by the Federal Bureau of Outdoor Recreation. Though such amounts are usually matched on a fifty-fifty basis by state, local, and private groups, an additional $300,000 of federal funds is coming from HUD's Community Development Authority.

While it is apparently legal, here is a situation where the federal government is taking the rap for 80 percent of the swimming pool and park complex instead of the usual 50 percent. And that's not counting the spectacular 4-foot surf.

But Salt Lake City doesn't have the only waves on the docket. Similar projects have been approved for construction in Kentucky and Mississippi, according to Bureau of Outdoor Recreation officials.

Why are these machines funded at all? A project spokesman told us that the surf-making should help keep Salt Lake City citizens home where they belong now that the energy crunch has made gasoline expensive: "Residents will no longer need to jump in their campers and travel 300 miles to feel the rushing water of Flaming Gorge."

As community development funds, under the law, must go primarily to low- and moderate-income citizens, either the owners of the campers are suddenly impoverished, or the rationale is of questionable validity.

*

In the last few years the spending psychology of the inflation victim has become a staple argument for the big spender in Congress. Whether it's a building, a dam, a weapons system, a highway, it's "Buy now; it will save you billions later."

Rarely do people stop to think that succumbing to the common inflation sickness may be one of the very things that's driving up prices. Spenders will recall any number of happy experiences when the Congress or some business went ahead with a big investment and was bailed out by inflation.

"Rockefeller Center in New York City was built in the thirties," they say. "Build it today and it would cost at least ten times as much." Or, "We built Dulles Airport just in time. If we'd waited until today, the cost would have been out of sight."

The argument then proceeds to considering the estimated price of an aircraft carrier or huge dam today. The high inflation rate is applied, exaggerated, and compounded. Senators are warned: "O.K. Postpone this expenditure. Five years from now it will cost you twice as much."

In rebuttal, you can argue till the cows come home that there's no reason to construct the aircraft carrier or dam at all. That five years from now the situation may have changed and you may find you don't want it.

But there's another much more telling rebuttal that is rarely considered, because it's technical and hard to understand—if you assume a high rate of inflation, you have to assume also a high opportunity cost for money. This is another way of saying that interest rates (as they are doing now) tend to rise to reflect inflation in full, and then some.

So that, instead of repeating in simple-minded fashion that a $100-million building will cost $200 million at a later date, you recognize that $100 million, *not spent but saved* and invested by the government for the taxpayers at the going rate of interest, will, under the most predictable circumstances, provide the $200 million at the same later date. And your option to spend, not spend at all, or spend in a less costly way will still be alive.

By taxing money out of the private sector and investing it in the public sector, we choke off private investment, which is likely to be more productive than public investment because it must meet the test of the marketplace. This is especially true in periods of economic growth.

Indeed, much federal spending is productive. And it is certainly true that there are needs of our society that can only be met by the federal government.

But federal spending has an astonishing, dangerous momentum, like a snowball rolling down a hill. It gets bigger and bigger and goes faster and faster. The pressure for spending for the millions who become addicted to federal programs is so intense that it sweeps the silly and even immoral programs along with the good and the necessary. Federal spending becomes an end in itself, a way to "keep the economy moving," so that "we're at high tide and all the ships are afloat." Spend right up to the point where there are jobs for everyone all the time.

This philosophy is now at last under serious political challenge, and it's about time.

(7)

Myths and Realities

IF YOU'RE A SENATOR struggling in committee or on the floor
of the Senate to reduce a spending program, you can expect to
be hit with a series of arguments that are very often the same
regardless of the appropriation under discussion. There is one in
particular that comes up again and again: you are cutting out
spending which will help the poor and unfortunate, the handicapped, the ill, the elderly. If you cut the budget, the little guy
will suffer.

But is this true? Is there any proof that it is so?

We queried the Library of Congress, the General Accounting
Office, the Brookings Institution, the Congressional Budget
Office, the Advisory Commission on Intergovernmental Relations, the American Enterprise Institute, the Tax Foundation,
and the Institute for Research on Poverty at the University of
Wisconsin to find if there were any good general studies detailing
the income distribution of federal spending. The answer, universally, was *no*. There were no studies, let alone good studies.

On the other side of the coin, let's take a look at analyses of
distribution, by income class, of tax expenditures. Don't duck
that forbidding term tax expenditures. It can cost you plenty.
When another person's taxes are reduced or eliminated, it means
your taxes will be increased. So, when the government gives an
exemption from personal income taxes to the first $20,000 of
income to thousands of Americans living abroad, that action

costs the Treasury hundreds of millions a year. It has the same effect on you as a taxpayer as if the government had spent that hundreds of millions of dollars. That is a tax expenditure. The following table shows that 76 percent of tax expenditures went to those with incomes in excess of $50,000 and only 2 percent to those with $10,000 or less.

Adjusted Gross Incomes	Percentage Distribution
$0–10,000 (about 50% of the population)	2.0
$10–20,000	3.3
$20–30,000	4.0
$30–50,000	14.7
$50,000 and over (about 1.5% of population)	76.0

Some individual studies of specific spending programs come out with similar results.

If you examine spending, agency by agency, and ask the question, "How much of this goes to the poor?" you will see that the bulk of the funds go to those with the political muscle and the economic power to push for them. The poor run interference, the well-to-do score the touchdowns. The blind, halt, lame, and impoverished are not ordinarily seen viewing the pictures at the National Gallery of Art or getting the research and development grants from NASA, Defense, or the National Science Foundation, nor are they generally visible at the higher levels of the government bureaucracy. On the following page is my off-the-cuff, rule-of-thumb estimate of the proportion of money spent to benefit the poor by major agencies.

Using generous estimates, it looks as if from $115 to $120 billion goes to the needy, out of a total of $531 billion. It would be useful to make a more accurate determination of Social Security, which constitutes a right for all and a vital need for many.

While labor, education, and training funds may be said to go to the poor only, there is little indication that they have improved conditions. The unemployment rate for black teenagers remains as high, if not higher, than ever. No dent seems to have been

Unit	FY 1980 Estimate in Billions	Comment
Legislative Branch	$1.3 billion	Virtually no funds to poor.
The Judiciary	$0.619	Virtually no funds to poor.
Executive Office of the President	$0.089	Virtually no funds to poor.
Funds Appropriated to the President	$5.1	Foreign Aid. $2.4 is military, $1.3 is multilateral, and $1.3 is bilateral. A generous estimate is that 20% of the $2.6 gets to the poor ($320 million).
Agriculture	$18.4	$6.9 is for food stamps. Another $3.5 is for special milk, food, and nutrition. 75% to poor equals $7.5 to $8 billion.
Commerce	$3.2	Virtually none of this goes directly to the poor. EDA funds may have some long-term trickle-down effects.
Defense	$122.7	None of the R&D and procurement funds go to the poor. If 15% of the $26 billion personnel funds go to the poor who have enlisted and are in the lower grades, $3.9 billion could be attributed.
Energy	$8.9	Very little for the poor.
HEW	$199.4	$101 billion of this is for Social Security. Another $15.7 billion is for the disabled. Another $15 billion or so is for assistance, disabled coal miners, etc. On grounds that Social Security recipients have average incomes lower than the society as a whole, about one-third could be said to go to the poor along with about $30–35 billion of the remaining HEW funds. Rough es-

Unit	*FY 1980 Estimate in Billions*	*Comment*
HEW (*cont.*)		timate to the poor—$75–80 billion.
Housing	$10.6	If 80% of housing assistance funds and one-third of Community Development gets to the poor, then about $5.8 billion of the total, or 55% of the department's funds, go to the poor.
Interior	$3.8	Very few, if any, of these funds go directly to the poor.
Justice	$2.5	Very little for the poor.
Labor	$24.5	$13.1 billion of this is outlays from the unemployment trust fund and $11 billion is for training. Estimate, 75%, or $18 billion, to the needy.
State	$1.7	Almost nothing for the poor.
Transportation	$15.8	Little or nothing.
Treasury	$69.9	Little or nothing.
EPA	$4.6	Little or nothing.
GSA	$0.131	Little or nothing.
NASA	$4.6	Little or nothing.
VA	$20.5	$11.1 billion for pensions and $5.4 billion for medical care, although neither service-connected disability nor hospital care has an effective means test, must go in considerable portion to the needy. Arbitrarily putting it at 50%.
ICC, FCC, NLRB, SEC, CPSC, and other independent agencies	$27.9	Virtually nothing.
Bureau of Indian Affairs	$0.65	$300 million

made in the rise of crime in the cities or in the horrendous living conditions.

Admittedly, things might have become much worse without some of the public programs. But, in general, they do not primarily aid the lowest income group. Seventy-five to 80 percent goes to those who are not in need.

Some will argue that funds for defense, highways, foreign affairs, police protection, and so forth, benefit all segments of society and that therefore some proportion, say 20 percent, of the DOD or DOT or State Department allocations or interest on debt funds should be counted in.

But it is difficult to argue that the $45 billion for interest on the national debt benefits the poor in any meaningful way; in fact those payments must be skewed to the very-high-income groups.

What is almost never acknowledged in all the arguments is the blockbuster effect of inflation—induced in part by federal spending—on the poor. Food stamps, in spite of their demeaning aspect and the abuse and fraud they inevitably bring on, by and large ease the effect of inflation on the very poor. The deep poor get some relief from hunger. It's the *near poor* who get hit right between the eyes.

As for other necessities—shelter, fuel, transportation (especially for the working poor), and clothing—inflation is cruel indeed. It's an annoyance and inconvenience for the well-to-do. For the poor it can be heartbreaking. Only a small number of the poor and near poor are helped by federally assisted housing, as we shall show later. Far more are hurt to the extent that federal programs drive up the cost of all housing, along with everything else we have to buy.

The hard fact is that our economy has been inflated in large part by improvident federal spending, and the poor and near poor are the primary victims.

Take our city rehabilitation and our housing programs for telling examples.

This country has a mammoth urban problem. Crime, poverty,

sickening living conditions, and extensive unemployment represent a signal failure for the nation. What should we do about it? The automatic knee-jerk reaction of both presidents and congressmen has been: use the marvelous resources of the country to restore, rebuild, clean up, and revive our cities. A Marshall plan.

It's an appealing slogan. The Marshall Plan was an example of unparalleled generosity paying off and paying off big. After World War II, Europe and Japan were heaps of rubble, their factories bombed out of existence, their highways and rail terminals devastated. Much of the free world seemed on the brink of collapse into despair and either communism or a revived fascism. Then the United States moved in with the Marshall Plan. Result: five years and $13 billion later there was an economic miracle. Seventeen countries—a total population larger than that of the United States—had been resurrected and were on their way to a far brighter economic life than they had ever enjoyed. The Marshall Plan was a smashing success.

If $13 billion could do it then, why not try it again, here and now, for American cities?

Let's consider. The Marshall Plan cost $2.6 billion a year for five years. What are we spending now on our cities? We are spending $85 billion a year! That's $425 billion every five years. More than *thirty times* the Marshall Plan. Even allowing for inflation the taxpayer is pouring more than ten times as many dollars into our American cities as went to Europe and Japan. If money were the answer, those cities would be gleaming, beautiful examples of the good life.

If you put it another way, a recent Brookings study found that, in 1957, taking a selected group of fifteen typical large cities, the federal government spent $1 for every $100 that was raised by the cities themselves. By 1975 the federal government was spending $47.50 for each $100 these cities, on the average, raised for their own resources, and since then the federal contribution has *doubled.*

What has been the result of this massive infusion? Dr. Richard Nathan of the Brookings Foundation has recently completed a study that shows that some of our cities have improved over the past twenty years—generally those in the Southwest and some in the Southeast. But his findings show that a large proportion of the big cities of the Northeast and Midwest have actually deteriorated further.

The criteria on which he based this judgment were age of housing, level of poverty, and the movement of the population. Obviously, the exodus of large numbers of citizens is a vital negative factor, indicating as it does a loss of economic opportunities.

There you have it: the most explosive increase in federal spending to improve urban life anywhere, anytime in history, has resulted in an almost complete failure.

Why the failure? Much of the money did not go to assist the poor. The community development program is a good example. This multibillion-dollar-a-year effort was designed by law to help those with low and moderate incomes. But where did the money go? More of it actually went to that one-fourth of the population that belonged to the highest income bracket according to the census in 1975 than to the one-fourth in the lowest income census tracts. In 1976 it was even more outrageous. That year, *50 percent* more money went to the highest income group (a finding from a study by the National Association of Housing and Rehabilitation Officials, published 1977).

But that's just a start. Billions were being and continue to be spent in ways that aggravate the hardships of the poor. Federal highway money, the old urban renewal program, and the new urban development action grants persistently bulldoze the dwellings of the poor, replacing their homes with freeways that help commuters to get out of town more easily, or with shiny office buildings, luxury hotels, or top-dollar condominiums.

For several years I have been chairman of both the Senate Banking, Housing, and Urban Affairs Committee and the Appropriations Committee that allocates the money for housing and most of the urban development programs. Time after time we have fought the battle to direct the more than $3.5 billion we spend every year for community development to the low-income people for whom the program was created. But we can never persuade a majority of senators and representatives on the committees to target the money in that direction.

It is especially difficult to persuade House members, because some of them have very few low-income citizens in their districts. Furthermore, the poor, especially the minority poor, vote less frequently, write seldom, and almost never phone or directly confront their congressmen or senators. Few of them would dream of asking for an appointment to talk turkey with any elected representative.

As for the federally assisted housing program, it is little short of a disaster. The cost is in the tens of millions and yet year after year the housing of impoverished Americans remains a national disgrace.

There is one major reason for this that is more the fault of the liberals than the conservatives. Liberals have the mythical notion that no American should have to pay more than 25 percent of his income for housing. Then they reduced that figure by providing a series of exceptions whereby hundreds of thousands who occupy housing units pay less than 25 percent, many only 15 percent, and some literally nothing.

This works a terrible inequity because the liberals have also been able to maintain on the books an eligibility standard for public housing assistance that includes those whose incomes are in the range of 80 percent of the *median* income in the community. The result is that tens of millions of Americans, not just the poorest sector, are eligible for housing assistance. Some estimate it as 40 percent of our citizens!

What happens? The vast majority of the truly poor are left out. They often live in miserable housing conditions and pay 40 or 50 percent of their meager incomes for the pitiful housing they get, while, because of the eligibility rules, families earning $12,000 can move into public housing and pay half as much rent as the families living on $5,000 and under.

The situation is worsened by pressure from labor unions and builders to put the available federal money into new housing rather than into remodeling the old. They constitute two powerful and effective lobbies, and they usually win out.

If more existing housing were used, the saving could be immense. Several billions would be salvaged if half the eligible families were put into used and half into new housing, instead of putting two-thirds into the new and only one-third into the used.

As for home ownership assistance, the following tables give some idea of where the money goes.

As you can see, except for rural housing, which splits fifty-fifty between lower- and upper-income groups, 65 to 99 percent of the funds from the home ownership spending programs goes to those with incomes above $10,000. With respect to home ownership tax expenditures, 96 percent of all the funds goes to those with over $10,000 a year. It is only in the rental programs that the median income of those participating is below $10,000.

*

There's another prevalent myth that billions poured into new educational facilites and more sophisticated teaching programs will produce a better-educated population. I am not arguing with the conviction that has become part of the American faith that the salvation of the country, as well as its individual citizens, lies in better education. Yet it cannot be denied that in the last decade or so, scholastic aptitude and general literacy have deteriorated. There may be many complicated reasons for this, but one thing is sure—we have wasted a fortune and need a great deal more intelligence in determining how to spend our education funds in the future.

From 1964 through 1978 this country increased the amount

Median Income Level of Participants in Rental Housing Spending Programs

Program	Median Income Level
Public housing	$3691
Section 8:	
New construction/substantial rehabilitation	4376
Existing housing	3506
Section 236	6285
Rent supplement	3544

Source: Department of Housing and Urban Development. Estimates are for participants in September 1977, except for the Section 8 estimates, which are for participants in June 1977.

Percentage Distribution of Home Ownership Spending Program Benefits by Income Class

Income Class (thousands)	Interest Subsidy Sec. 235	FHA Credit	Programs		Rehabilitation Sec. 312
			Rural Housing	GNMA Tandem	
0 to $10	19	6	50	1	35
$10 to $20	80	67	35	46	47
$20 to $50	1	27	15	51	17
$50 and over	0	0	0	2	1

Sources: Department of Housing and Urban Development and the Farmers Home Administration, Department of Agriculture.

Percentage Distribution of Home Ownership Tax Expenditures by Income Class, Fiscal Year 1977

Expanded Income Class (thousands)	Mortgage Interest Deduction	Property Tax Deduction	Deferral of Capital Gains Tax
0 to $10	2.0	1.9	4.0
$10 to $20	24.5	19.4	42.8
$20 to $50	61.2	53.0	48.3
$50 and over	12.3	25.7	4.8

Source: Department of the Treasury.

we poured into education by a smashing 400 percent. The funds came from every level of government. Allowing fully for inflation, and for a somewhat larger number of students, the per-capita expenditure in education dollars has virtually doubled. If money alone had been the answer, we would have been graduating the smartest young people on the globe.

But what has been the result? Ever since 1964 the scholastic aptitude test scores of our children have gone one way—*down*. Every year. Bigger and brighter, beautiful new schools built in one community after another, new libraries, better-paid and better-qualified teachers, the new visual aids, the dramatic reduction of class size—where has all this got us? Evidently nowhere. Not even running in place. Consider the following table.

School Year	SAT Verbal All Candidates	SAT Math All Candidates	Amount Spent per Pupil Allowing Fully for Inflation, 1976–77 PP
1963–64	475	498	$875
1965–66	471	496	987
1967–68	466	494	1135
1969–70	460	488	1268
1971–72	450	482	1412
1973–74	440	478	1519
1975–76	429	470	1597
1976–77	429	471	1578*

*Estimate
Source: National Center for Education statistics.

Look at the scholastic aptitude figures and correlate the money with the descending scores. What it says is that the more we spent from 1963–64 to 1976–77 on our children's education, the dumber they got. A perfect correlation is 1.0. The ultimate negative correlation is minus 1.0. If there is no correlation at all it is simply 0. It is rare in measuring any kind of human endeavor that you get a higher than plus or minus 0.6 or 0.7 correlation. A 0.9 correlation is almost unheard of. Yet this one is 0.95, running awfully close to a perfect negative correlation.

The motive for spending more on education is excellent. Nothing is more important for a country than the training, the skill, the ability of its people. We depend on these qualities far more than on natural resources or the quantity of our factories, farms, and military forces. England, for instance, a tiny country with a relatively small population, pitiful resources, and an urgent need to import almost all its food and raw materials, dominated the globe for two hundred years largely because of the quality of its education. And it was not until the United States instituted universal education, and prolonged the period each child must go to school, that it became the world leader.

When our leadership seemed threatened by the spectacular Russian Sputnik thrust into space, we responded with the massive federal aid to education I have described.

But it hasn't worked. Why?

There are many alibis. Television keeps children from studying or just plain reading. Parents have lost the punch to force their children to study, and they pay little attention to the schools. The deterioration of the family unit has worked its evils. The present permissive society has put a taboo on the sort of punishment and discipline that got results in the past. In our welfare society many feel they can get by whether they work or not. If you don't get a job, you will always get food stamps and enough money to survive.

But none of these alibis really covers the deteriorating situation. It may be that the greater size of our schools—the abolishing of the local, more personal schoolhouse—has made many parents feel they aren't needed or wanted for the cooperation that is essential in the motivation of their children. In an earlier era most parents would serve some time on the school board, they knew their child's teacher, and it mattered to both parent *and* teacher whether Jane and Johnny could spell and do the arithmetic tables. These things have to be learned by rote, and the notion that this generation is too sophisticated and advanced for rote learning is probably responsible for the functional illiteracy of an appalling 13 percent of our seventeen-year-olds—not to mention some of our college graduates. (Students in one of our leading business schools are required to take "expository writing," which includes not only grammar and spelling but also brushing up on careful and intelligent reading.)

Rand, the California think tank, made a study of four federal programs that poured money into education, examining 283 local projects run on government money. They found there was *zero* correlation between the amounts spent and the success of the programs.

If not money, if not the big new "comprehensive" high and junior high schools, with all varieties of expensive equipment and, theoretically, better-trained teachers, what does make an education program work? In my opinion the answer is local interest, local enthusiasm, and local commitment. If the community has no emotional stake in a program, the federal money goes right down a rat hole.

What this suggests, and suggests strongly, is that the federal government stop providing funds *directly* for education and filter it down through local governments—giving the tax authority over to them. If the states and local governments choose simply not to fund one of these programs by going through the grief of raising local taxes for it, then that program is obviously going to be a failure.

Among federal programs, those that fund vocational education programs providing young people with specific skills can have a reasonable payoff. And they usually have powerful local support. Both business and the students themselves can see that here is an expenditure that promotes a trained work force and gives young men and women the hope of earning a good wage.

But educational spending that provides a student with no marketable skill and such a poor capacity to read and write and do simple mathematics that he or she can't pass competency tests are a waste of the student's time and the taxpayers' money.

Unfortunately, there are indications that the semiliterate holders of college degrees are increasing. More money won't solve the problem. What could really help are tougher college admission and graduation standards. And again, unfortunately, there is a tendency now, in many colleges, to eliminate admission requirements entirely. The tests that a student must take to enter an institution of higher education have always been the spur for both parent and teacher to keep an adolescent—with all the distractions at hand—on the path of learning.

This is a matter cured not by money but by judgment. In fact, less federal money might even be useful. It might eliminate some of those who should never go to college at all and would be more productive and happier in another situation.

Both younger and older Americans are beginning to learn how mythical the value of a college education is per se. It's time to make it a real value again, worth striving for in primary and secondary schools, and truly worth federal aid. Then we might keep the basic intelligence and literacy of our nation from going under.

How They Pull It Off

A PROTESTING CITIZENRY indicates again and again in many ways that it wants the spending slowed down. How can it be that 535 elected representatives and a President who is popularly elected combine to continue to impose such an immense burden of spending that has to be paid for by taxes?

Does the public really want a slowdown? In the 1978 election, the dominant theme was "elect me to hold down spending." The same song was consistently sung by Democrats and liberals as well as Republicans and conservatives.

The polls also indicated that a big majority of Americans in every income class, whites and blacks, young and old, conservative and liberal, agreed on one thing: government spending was too big and should be cut. The reason for this is clear: taxes. Fifty years ago, back in the 1930s, the average American paid less than 10 percent of his personal income in local, state, and federal taxes. By 1940 he was paying 20 percent. Today he is paying more than 40 percent. Wars and revolutions—including our own Revolution—have been sparked off by lesser woes. Then add the fact that federal taxes, big and burdensome as they are and have been, have not matched federal spending; result, a massive deficit and a swelling national debt which costs nearly $60 billion a year in interest. And, worst of all, for the first time in our peacetime history, a persisting, growing inflation threatens every American.

True, federal spending isn't the only cause of inflation, but it's a major cause, especially when the economy nears the full use of its resources and the deficits continue unabated.

Public revolt against the situation is coming out loud and clear even if in crude ways, such as the surprising upset victory of Proposition 13 in California. That initiative won by a smashing two to one, though it was opposed by a popular governor, by the major corporations, the news media, the unions, and just about every other organized group. Also, there was another, more moderate and "respectably" supported economy referendum on the same ballot.

The sudden flash of support in 1978 and early 1979 for a constitutional convention that would force Congress to balance the budget is another loud and unmistakable call for holding down spending.

A constitutional convention could become a nightmare. The last one was held in 1789. It tore up the articles of confederation and gave the country a brand new, entirely different Constitution. That Constitution has rightly become venerated as the best protection of the freedoms and the most viable framework for a balance of political power that any country, anywhere, has ever put together. It came from the conjunction of remarkably wise and prescient Founding Fathers at a time when both desire for freedom and political understanding of the abuses of political power were ascendant. But a constitutional convention could tear that charter to pieces. It could knock out the Bill of Rights. Of course that might not happen and probably wouldn't, but why take the chance? In my judgment, Congress should require itself to balance the budget by means that I shall describe in a later chapter of this book.

Yet the rapid approval in state after state of an amendment that would mandate a balanced federal budget—even when that balancing might deny those very states the happy largesse they have been receiving—provides a message that even the politically deaf have to hear.

With the will of their constituents so clearly expressed, why do elected officials continue to open the spending spigots full blast year after year?

One way to answer that is to analyze how federal funds are cozened, teased, pressed, even bullied out of Congress and the executive branch of the government. Who does it, and how do they do it? We might start with a few examples.

The Mayors and the Governors

On the wall of my office I have a few words of advice from a very bright Pennsylvanian named Herbert Denenberg. He served as a swashbuckling insurance commissioner for several years to the consternation of the insurance industry and the delight of Pennsylvania consumers. He ran for public office a few times, unfortunately without winning. When asked by prospective constituents what they could do to get what they wanted, he replied: "Do three things: get informed, get organized, and get tough."

This is precisely what the pro-spending forces have done and what the pro-economy forces haven't even begun to think about. The result has been that petitioners for public money win almost every contest.

Mayors and governors are startlingly successful at this. Somehow members of Congress are more than a little leery of their political power. They fear that a mayor will avenge any legislator's refusal of public money by delivering an entire city's vote against him in the next election. This threat seems to work, though in reality it's a hollow bluff. There is no group of constituents that a member of Congress can more freely defy than the elected officials within his state. The reason? That elected official, just like the congressman, has to run for reelection too, and he can't afford to alienate anyone, especially the supporters of a senator or representative who has won an election. Mayors are, uniformly, paper tigers.

The mayor of Milwaukee, Henry Maier, is a remarkably able politician. In spite of opposition from both of the city's newspapers, he has won election after election with margins approaching 80 percent. He has organized an alliance of cities in Wisconsin to pressure Wisconsin senators and congressmen and state legislators to vote for more spending for Milwaukee and other Wisconsin cities.

A few weeks before the 1976 election, when I was up for reelection, Maier's Alliance of Wisconsin Cities passed a resolution denouncing me for failing to support their proposals for federal funds. That attack on me was empty and ineffective; in fact, I think it increased my winning margin in the cities. People seemed to feel that here was one sign that Proxmire really meant business about holding down spending.

The mayor had tried another tactic a few months before. In the paycheck envelopes of thousands of Milwaukee city employees he had enclosed a note urging them to circulate petitions to get me to vote for revenue sharing. This was a more than $6-billion-a-year giveaway to the states and cities which I have consistently opposed because the federal government has a deficit, *not* a revenue, to share, and, because it was a handout, requires no accountability at all.

In return, I addressed a public statement to the mayor:

> The revenue sharing bill is an absolute, lead pipe cinch to become law. There is no way Wisconsin can miss getting its revenue sharing funds.
>
> Consider: the bill has already passed the House by a smashing 361 to 35 vote. It is sure to pass the Senate, with the Proxmire vote in opposition, by an overwhelming majority. The President will enthusiastically sign it into law . . .
>
> So why does the Mayor spend a few hundred dollars of the Milwaukee taxpayers' money to send out some 10,000 notices that tell Milwaukee city employees to get on my back by going house to house with their petitions to change my mind? . . .
>
> Now, Mayor, there's not a distant echo of a whisper of an outside chance that a single Milwaukeean will lose a nickel. That's because the revenue sharing is going to pass. And you know it . . .

I am trying to amend the revenue sharing bill so that the states will be accountable to their taxpayers as they are not, now, for revenue sharing.

My first amendment would send the revenue sharing back to Wisconsin federal income taxpayers as a refund. The state could, and almost surely would, then appropriate all or part of the funds for revenue sharing, but the state legislators would have to pass a law and assume responsibility to the Wisconsin taxpayers for doing so.

Why shouldn't the Wisconsin taxpayer who pays for every nickel of this revenue sharing through his federal income tax have a voice in where the Wisconsin-allocated money is going?

My second amendment would bring revenue sharing into compliance with the General Accounting Office recommendation—made after a careful study—by requiring that general revenue sharing to the larger units of government be independently audited and the results of the audit be reported fully and promptly to the press and taxpayer.

A two-year study by the League of Women Voters found that revenue sharing funds, nationally, are spent without any accountability and that no one at the federal, state or local level can account for where most of these funds go.

Since that response to Mayor Maier, I have decided that the federal government simply cannot afford revenue sharing at all. The federal government has no revenue to share. The states and local governments should only spend that money which they raise directly from their own taxpayers, and for which they have to account to their taxpayers.

The governors, too, do their share of arm twisting. Governor Hugh Carey of New York suggested in his 1979 inaugural address that the federal government try to balance the budget, looking to New York State, where, according to him, "government is no longer a growth industry." "Let the federal government practice the frugality of New York," said Carey, conveniently forgetting that New York received more federal aid in 1978 than any state, and among the industrial states was first at the federal trough for money, surpassed on a per-capita basis only by five very small, mostly rural states.

What makes Governor Carey's position especially ironic is that it was his masterful work on the Congress in 1975 and again in 1978 in collaboration with two gifted New York senators that persuaded the Congress for the first time to go to the rescue of an American city in financial straits.

In New York City's case, I'm convinced that the present $1.7 billion federal guarantee will be paid off. But the precedent could haunt the country and its taxpayers. Having said yes to New York City, how can we say no to any other city or state in deep financial trouble? Throughout our history, our cities and states have been remarkably prudent in managing their budgets, and one big reason for this has been the specter of default and bankruptcy and ruinous consequences for both citizens and elected officials. Now that New York City has been bailed out—not once but twice—that line may be harder to hold. (For more on the New York situation, see Chapter 10.)

Such governors as Jerry Brown in California and Bruce Babbit in Arizona also beat their breasts during their 1979 inaugural campaigns and called on the federal government to follow their lead in holding down spending. But in the years I have been in Washington, I have never once heard or seen a governor who has come to Washington, or written or called, asking that any spending program which he could possibly use in his state be cut back. Both governors and mayors testifying before our Senate Banking Committee invariably ask for more money.

And for one reason or another—but primarily because of the illusionary threat that they can hurt members of Congress in the next election—they seem to have a way of getting what they want.

The Educators

Here is a big clout too. I have already discussed the immense increase in the last decade in federal aid to education. Until 1949 this was strictly limited to the GI bill for veterans education and relatively few minor programs involving some vocational and agricultural training. But Congress, under the leadership of Senator Taft, decided we had to do something about the young people who couldn't share equally in the American dream of hard work and study leading to a better life when they came from poor states that couldn't afford the same quality of education as the well-to-do states. Then Sputnik challenged our math and our science, and we were off to the races.

The pressure for more and more millions is building up. The educators follow the advice of Herb Denenberg which I quoted. They are generally informed. They know their programs. They are organized. Finally, they know how to get tough. The National Education Association and the American Federation of Teachers both represent thousands of voters. They can turn on a letter-writing campaign, and they appear in Washington constantly to beard their congressmen in their offices and say, "How about it? Do you support us or not?" They are experts at working with congressional staff members, many of whom come from their own ranks and are in turn adept at turning senators and representatives around on the crucial votes at the right time.

As I noted earlier, the results have not justified the costs: lower SAT scores dismay us year after more expensive year. Federal assistance now enables close to half the college-age population to acquire some higher education. Assistance is provided regardless of income, through "basic opportunity grants" and scholarships. What's the trouble with this largesse? Plenty!

It means that the lower-income people who don't go to college subsidize with their taxes the children of the higher-income people who do. It also means we may be wasting millions on students who get no real advantage—American dream notwithstanding— out of those four years of subsidized education.

In a rare and admirable move, the University of Wisconsin (at Racine and Kenosha) made it a requirement that students, before they could graduate, had to pass a test to show minimum competence in writing, mathematics, and library research. The reaction of some students was, "The nerve of the University. I'm going to transfer to a technical school."

The Military Lobby

Here's one with a huge but varying back-up. This lobby trades in power that it adapts to suit a congressman's vulnerability. For any legislator who has a large military base or a great deal of defense work in his state or district, the appeal is direct and simple. Such a congressman is often a very easy mark. For example, one of the most respected members of the Senate comes from a state that is awash with defense contracts. He is in truth an ardent supporter of the Strategic Arms Limitation treaties. Yet he is devastating in committee and when working the Senate floor in his support of individual weapons systems to be produced in *his* state, and for abolishing the Renegotiation Board and the Vinson-Trammel Act, which is trying to put a cap on the profits of defense contractors.

Even senators and congressmen whose states or districts are not much involved in defense contracts are vulnerable. "Do you want this great country of ours to be number two to the Russians?" ask the lobbyists. "Do you want us to be humiliated again and again because we have to knuckle under to a superior military force?" And, of course, every member of Congress has his veterans' organizations at home who reflect these views. They are organized, they write, and they vote.

A surprising number of senators are suckers for a particular kind of weapons system or even for a favorite branch of the military. A large proportion of them have served in one or another of the armed services. If they have flown fighters or bombers, they will usually vote for more planes and more costly planes. Some senators have a weakness for ships. The sea may be their hobby, their love. But it can cost a bundle for obsolete craft.

The prime deterrent, of course, to cutting down military spending is that national security is such an ultimate value. "What good is anything else in this country if we're going to be destroyed by a more powerful nation?"

The result is that senators who would argue over every dollar of a food stamp or housing program have a complete blind spot when it comes to defense. Suddenly dollars don't mean anything. So it costs a billion or ten billion more—"It might save the nation!" When this level of panic thinking predominates, there can be no limit on a military proposal. As long as we can persuade our colleagues that a program might be worth funding at fifty million but becomes questionable at sixty million and ridiculous at one hundred million, we have a rational basis for decision. But when a number of senators believe that a certain weapons system is good at any price—no matter what—our only chance is a presidential veto.

When we do win a victory over the military lobbies, such as our successful battle against the B-1 bomber and occasional wins against bigger aircraft carriers, it's almost invariably with strong support from the President. President Carter deserves the fullest credit for stopping the insane waste of building another B-1 bomber. Without his opposition, we would have been in for a full two-hundred-billion spending sponsored by a huge, lopsided majority in both the House and the Senate.

Let me describe how that disaster was almost perpetrated against the taxpayer by the big defense lobby. Rockwell International bankrolled a classic PR campaign in support of the B-1 bomber program. Advertisements were placed in the *Wall Street Journal* (4 times), the *New York Post, Seattle Post Intelligencer,* and *Seattle Times* (6 times), the *Providence Evening Bulletin* and *Providence Journal, Wilmington Morning News* and *Wilmington Evening Journal* (3 times), the *Atlanta Constitution, Atlanta Journal, St. Louis Post-Dispatch,* and *St. Louis Globe Democrat* (6 times), the *Springfield, Illinois, Journal Register* and *Chicago*

Daily News (13 times), and in many other major newspapers throughout the country.

In addition, Rockwell used a number of other devices which *may* have been written off, for tax purposes, as business expenses, and thus may have been borne by American taxpayers:

- Rockwell employees toured the country to speak with newspaper editors about supporting the B–1.
- Major advertising went into aerospace publications such as *Aviation Week, Space Technology,* and the *Air Force Magazine.*
- Dues or membership fees were paid to pro-B–1 organizations such as the Air Force Association, American Security Council, Aerospace Industries Association, Council of Space Industry Association, Electronic Industries Association, National Aeronautics Association, National Security Industrial Association, and the National Aerospace Service Association.
- Slides and films extolling the B–1 were produced and distributed. One, for example, was a film about the Rockwell chief test pilot on his first flight in the B–1, as distributed by Paramount Pictures.
- Research organizations and other public relations firms were given financial support either to publicize the merits of the bomber or to encourage lobbying in its behalf.
- Operation Common Sense was set up and funded by Rockwell in 1974 as an internal lobbying force designed to influence veterans' organizations, provide B–1 speakers for citizens' groups, counter anti-B–1 activities, and so forth.
- Letters were written to all Rockwell stockholders and employees recommending that they write to Congress in support of the B–1.

(PR and lobbying activities are a normal part of private enterprise and contribute to healthy debate on national issues. If, by any chance, however, they are supported by tax funds or claimed under government contracts, that means the taxpayer is financing a lobbying campaign against himself.)

As I said, the President saved the day. Theoretically the Congress enjoys the power of the purse, and the President, as Commander-in-Chief of the Armed Forces, has the power of the sword. In fact, the President, as the initiator of the budget, commands the fiscal heights. Even in the military area, Congress will rarely exceed the President's budget figure. We know he has a veto and can and will wield it.

Congress, maligned as it has been on spending, has reduced every President's budget in twenty-four of the last twenty-five years. The reductions have been grossly inadequate but represent some effort to cut down spending. The B–1 bomber affair suggests how critical presidential judgment is in the battle to hold the line against unwise, almost hysterical spending.

The Health Professionals

Remember when a hospital bed cost $9 a day? My father was a doctor in a very prosperous suburb of Chicago. Like every other doctor in those days before Medicare and Medicaid he did a lot of "charity" work. But his fees must have been as high as most. He was chief of staff of the local hospital, a Fellow of the American College of Surgeons, and had by far the best practice in town. His charges—hold your breath—were $10 for a house call at night, $5 for one in the daytime, $1 for an office visit, $25 to deliver a baby, and a little but not much more for a major operation!

Multiply that by ten to twenty and you have today's average charges. Allowing fully for inflation, the cost of getting sick has gone out of sight.

Federal programs are certainly a major reason. I voted for Medicare and would again. When you're over sixty-five, you're likely to be ill four times as often as when you are younger; your income has gone down, and charity treatment may not hurt the doctors but it doesn't do much for the pride of the patient—if (a big if) he or she can find such treatment. Medicare was indeed necessary.

How about Medicaid? This takes care of the poor at any age. I voted for that too. You get just as sick when you are poor as when you're well-off, and you can't afford the present prices of either doctors or hospitals.

But what was necessary for the old and the poor is now being pushed for everyone else, which would send an already immense federal cost soaring to the stars. The polls tell us that the vast majority of Americans want it. This could turn into another $100 billion burden, with rigid controls thrown in to boot, and a consequent deterioration in the quality of medical services.

The lobbying for universal health care is growing more insistent. The only thing that holds it back is division in the ranks of the health professionals. But when they decide they want it, they'll get it, and maybe they'll get it sooner than that.

Medicare and Medicaid were designed for the elderly and the impoverished, and in a compassionate and caring country these programs serve great objectives. But because there is no discipline to hold costs down, the fees charged to patients by doctors and hospitals have been immensely inflated, becoming a colossal burden on taxpayers who are pouring their money in to support such mammoth programs as Medicaid. There is no question that the doctors are getting very rich indeed out of our medical programs. They now enjoy the highest average compensation of any profession anywhere and anytime in history.

The Bankers

For twenty-two years I have served on the Senate Banking Committee, and since January of 1975 have been its chairman. During this span of time I have come to recognize the American Bankers Association as something close to an irresistible force vis-à-vis legislation affecting banks.

Bankers occupy a powerful position in our society; they are everywhere, in every congressional district, scores in every state —the total for the country comes to 16,000. Yet the congressional respect they inspire is far out of proportion to their numbers because of the money they control. They are usually, one might say, by definition, affluent themselves. And almost every member of Congress is in debt to some banker somewhere. In many cases those debts are directly related to the congressman's election. Directly or indirectly, they finance many a campaign. But even more important, a goodly portion of a senator's or representative's constituents are also beholden to the banker. He is a man who can be feared as well as respected.

This was brought home to me vividly one day when I was buttonholing senators to get them to support a bill which seemed to me in the interest of borrowers, lenders, and taxpayers generally. I approached a sensitive young Southern senator, identified the bill, and started to make my pitch. I'd barely started when he said, "Prox, don't waste your time. I'd love to help you but I have letters from twelve of my bankers opposing your legislation and there's no way I can support it even if it was the greatest thing since the adoption of the Constitution."

Twelve bankers! Their interests were special and selfish and self-serving. But they were the pillars of their communities—the establishment itself. A smart senator in either the South or the North would think twice before crossing them.

The American Bankers Association lobby continues to wield this sort of power in spite of one of the most negative and reactionary records in American politics. It has opposed every constructive suggestion to do anything about reforming our banking situation. Take them one by one:

- They opposed the Federal Reserve Act that gave this country the basis of monetary policy which the banks now say is the best in the world.
- They opposed federal deposit insurance, a law that has saved us from the periodic panics and widespread bank failures that plagued the country about every ten or fifteen years until 1933, when the Federal Deposit Insurance Corporation (FDIC) took effect. Now they say the FDIC is essential and they're all for it.
- They opposed the Truth in Lending Law, the Fair Credit Reporting Bill, and anti-redlining legislation.

Sometimes when the American Bankers' representatives come before our committee, I challenge them to name a single constructive piece of legislation they have ever supported. I'm still waiting for the answer.

They continue to get their way. Until recently, they influenced Congress and the President to prohibit banks from paying any interest on their demand deposits, limiting the amount they pay on savings deposits, all of which kept the costs to the banks low, while freeing them completely from any restraint on the interest they can charge on the loans they make.

On top of all this, many of the bankers have the crust to tell the Congress and the President to require the Federal Reserve to pay interest on the funds the banks hold at the Fed, an operation that could result in paying the banks literally billions of dollars a year at the expense of the general taxpayer.

The Home Builders

This lobby represents literally thousands of builders, big and small, throughout the country, who want the government to spend more and more on housing. The amount is already immense—the cost to the federal government for building 200,000 housing units per year is about $7 billion.

But that's only a beginning. Like other home buyers, the government chooses to finance these units over a period of twenty years, on an average. With interest rates at the "normal" level they have attained in recent years, the financing cost is another $10 billion—making $17 billion in all. If we wanted to reduce the cost, we could make existing used houses available to those on the housing assistance rolls. But, of course, in that event the builders wouldn't get as much business.

They always do an excellent job of testifying before our banking committee. They do their homework. They are informed. They visit the office of each of the banking committee members. They talk to the senator. They talk to the senator's staff. They make sure that the builders in his home state visit the senator both at home and in Washington. They are always pleasant and friendly. If the senator disappoints them with a vote, they are just as friendly next time. They invite senators who sit on the Banking Committee to dinners and cocktail parties in Washington and in the home states, and often ask them to speak at their association's meetings.

For a Democrat who may not have much business support, they are especially welcome, because they are respected businessmen, usually in good standing with the local Chamber of Commerce, and if they approve the senator's voting record on housing, he can count on their support.

You can see why the Congress will vote billions for programs they push, though such programs may be highly inflationary and certainly a potentially immense tax burden.

But ask yourself, if you were a builder, would you do any different? Your livelihood depends on this prime customer—the federal government. And you can always make a good case for building more homes in the national interest.

And if you were a senator and these great good fellows—friendly, supportive, respected businessmen—simply asked you to consider the national interest—from their point of view—wouldn't you be tempted? (After all, you can always save the money somewhere else.)

Big Labor and Big Business

The builders, the defense contractors, and the public works enthusiasts can be tough lobbyists by themselves. But when they team up with organized labor, and they often do, then watch out.

Though business and labor have had long, tough fights that have bitterly divided the Senate and consumed weeks of filibuster hours—as with the labor law reform bill—they are apt to line up on the same side when it's a federal spending issue.

After a few years of fighting lost causes in the Senate, a senator learns he must, on any tough, divisive issue, line up his lobbying supporters and make sure they do the hard spadework of persuading other senators to his point of view. Any time he can line up labor, he's halfway home; if he can line up only organized business, he's also halfway home. But get them both, and he has it made. And if a senator wants more federal housing, that labor-builder coalition is easy to put together. This simple fact goes a long way in explaining the explosion of government spending in the last twenty-five years, for this coalition occurs in many areas beyond housing.

Cooperation between the AFL-CIO construction trades and the business-oriented builders is of course the classic example, with the latter going after the Republicans and conservatives and the former gathering in the Democrats and liberals. Many a senator will then be urged to support the additional spending by both camps. How can he resist? Does he want them *both* against him?

Under these circumstances, the merits of the case against spending have to be very powerful indeed to have any effect. When Johnny Schmidt, the head of the Wisconsin State AFL-CIO and an extraordinarily intelligent, knowing lobbyist, or some other Wisconsin labor leader, calls me from Milwaukee and says, "Bill, how about it? We need your vote. It means a lot to us," I remember that this is the organization that has supported me in election after election. I also remember how they have fought for the poor, the minorities, the uneducated. And that there are close to a million persons—including family members—who are in organized labor in Wisconsin. No one can come close to delivering that entire vote. But labor leadership is generally respected in Wisconsin, and it has earned that respect. When it supports an issue or a candidate, that support carries weight.

Sometimes I tell the Wisconsin labor leader no, sometimes yes. Sometimes I just say, "I'll think it over." On spending matters, my answer is usually negative, but having been through this for many years, I can understand the temptation to say yes. And how much stronger the temptation when both business and labor gang up on me.

The ironic, frustrating angle here is that the *individual* businessman deplores the fact that, with its budget of over $500 billion, the federal government represents a solid one-fifth of the entire gross national product. Businessmen realize what that is doing to taxes and to inflation. The individual laboring man feels the same way. Yet when organized business and organized labor move on Washington, they almost never reflect the sentiment of their individual members, but slap on their armor and ride into the fray to battle for government spending with a vengeance.

Spokesmen for the Chamber of Commerce and the National Association of Manufacturers (NAM) will appear before the Budget Committee or Joint Economic Committee and call for a tougher fiscal policy and a balanced budget. Ask them to be specific, and they will answer, "That's your job, Senator." Again and again I have urged the able former economist for the National Chamber of Commerce, Jack Carlson, and the intelligent expert for the NAM, George Hagedorn, to appear before the Appropriations Committee and oppose specific spending programs, anywhere in the budget. But they don't show up. And if organized labor has ever opposed any spending program, even in theory, I've never heard of it.

When it comes to programs that will enrich contractors and provide lucrative jobs to workers—the procurement of a multibillion-dollar weapons system or a gigantic national housing program—both industry and labor lobby for their own workers and their own trade associations. But if it's a project that doesn't involve money in their pockets, but will absorb the taxes of workingmen and businessmen alike, they couldn't care less; they are indifferent.

Such self-interest will never balance the budget, even with everyone in the land screaming for it.

Friends of the Inarticulate Poor

Here is the last but not least potent ingredient of what becomes literally a coalition of lobbyists putting pressure on the government to spend, and spend again.

The lobbyists for groups that directly represent the people who are supposed to benefit from federal spending—the "deserving poor"—are, individually, the salt of the earth.

Cushing Dolbeare, for instance, is a brilliant woman who fights for and gets funds that are supposed to replace slums with decent living quarters. She speaks for what she calls the Low Income Housing Coalition. For years she has supplied our banking committee with excellent, detailed information justifying her cause.

Roy Wilkins of the National Association for the Advancement of Colored People (NAACP), Vernon Jordan, and others have done equally praiseworthy promotion of housing assistance for blacks. Others do the same kind of careful, detailed work for the handicapped. Able, dedicated people lobby for the multibillion-dollar employment-training programs and the expensive health, education, and welfare programs.

These lobbyists are generally able to move senators to action because they are well informed and sincere in their motives. They are often paid little; and they put in many hours above and beyond the call of duty. They testify before our committees; they call on me and other senators in our offices, talking at length to our committee and personal staffs. They are compassionate and they have done their best to urge department personnel to administer the programs for *poor,* not middle-income, Americans.

These are the front-line troops that provide many of the visible arguments which justify the biggest appropriations.

Unfortunately the spending floodgates, once opened, are manipulated to permit a diversion of much of the public money to help those who don't need it. The rest of the coalition of lobbyists—mayors, governors, bankers, home builders, organized labor—all want their share. And because even this coalition has limits on how much it can extract from the budget, most of the spending—including the so-called social programs—goes to the already well-off rather than to the needy and impoverished.

I have already described, in Chapter 7, the inequities of the Community Development Program, specifically designed *by law* to help low- and moderate-income people. And the urban renewal program has on the whole simply bulldozed the dwellings of the poor and replaced them with urban facilities—such as offices, condominiums, and overhead expressways—for the middle and upper classes. Urban Development Action, a new name for the old urban renewal program, is taking the same devastating course, with the poor neighborhoods picking up a few scraps. CETA money has gone in large amounts to help mayors maintain their excess city employees (along with their substantial salaries) instead of employing and training disadvantaged young people.

The Hidden Lobby in the White House

Technically the executive branch is not legally allowed to lobby. In reality, the "legislative liaison" official and his staff do almost nothing else. If, for example, a senator proposes a reduction in a department's budget that would take its funds below the amount allocated in the President's budget, the secretary of that department will send his or her legislative liaison team into action. It is usually composed of assistant secretaries of the department, who are usually the best-informed people in government on the programs involved and have their friends and supporters in the Senate.

If it's a cut in the housing budget, the Secretary of the Department of Housing may get on the phone or come to the Senate offices with, "You can't do this to me!" or, "Do you realize what this reduction in funds could do to Milwaukee?"

Thus the business-labor-governor-mayor-friends-of-the-poor coalition gets additional mileage by a push from the Administration.

The Donors

Campaign contributors are almost universally on the spending side. They are organized to raise money for us, write us, call us, meet with us, and plead with us to spend the federal golden hoard for the programs they want. And in hundreds of cases they will vote for or against a member of Congress strictly on those grounds. This is an all-important factor that continues to send spending up and up. No one, and I mean no one, makes a campaign contribution to encourage a senator *not* to spend money.

Of course there are a few groups that contribute to a senator because they count on him to spend more money on a single, special program, such as the housing program. In this case, the builders, the savings and loan institutions, commercial banks, credit unions, AFL-CIO construction trades (including a number of unions), and the purveyors of lumber, cement, furnishings, and so forth, are after him. If a legislator happens to be on an appropriations committee in the House or Senate or on the Senate Banking Committee, then the money is laid on. Large contributions go to members of those committees who have jurisdiction over housing.

If you don't think this is a major reason why federally subsidized housing is in the tens of billions, you still believe in the tooth fairy and Santa Claus.

No, the campaign contributions are not bribes. They are fully disclosed. Some members of Congress take them and still vote against the desires of the donors. But that's not easy. Many senators agree with the California political powerhouse, Jesse Unruh, who called money the "mother's milk of politics."

With money, you can enter thousands of voters' homes on

television. Or write to tens of thousands who may agree with you on part of your voting record but were unaware of it. You can buy pamphlets extolling your virtues and hire hundreds to distribute them to voters in the remotest sections of your constituency. Without money your campaign goes nowhere; you stand mute, tongue-tied, with both hands behind your back, a punching bag for the cruelest kinds of distortions, if not actual lies, that your opponent aims at you. Money makes the difference between winning and losing in a close election. An underdog candidate who spends money wisely can beat a heavily favored opponent.

Money—mother's milk—is what you need, and, if you are a typical candidate, you think you need it more than you actually do. At this point, some swell guys come along and contribute $1000, maybe $5000. They all want the same thing: your vote on a certain spending program that will benefit their business or their union. These contributions can easily add up to half a million, or far more—just for one senator's campaign.

Senators are human beings with limited time and attention. When virtually all the pressure and the arguments, as well as all the contributions, come from the pro-spending segment a senator's response is not completely predictable, but it is likely to be in favor of his benefactors' favorite spending programs. Even if he hasn't actually promised (and there are some who don't sell out in the end), he wouldn't be human if he didn't feel gratitude, give those swell guys an ear, try to understand their cause, and try to give them credit for sincerely feeling that what they want is in the national interest.

No group sends him campaign money to persuade him to hold down the budget.

The factor that really buttons it up is that about one-third of the senators have been through a campaign within the preceding two years. They have not forgotten the "mother's milk" that helped them get elected. Another third are facing a reelection campaign in less than two years. Every day brings them closer to the polls and reminds them how they will need contributions and how much easier it will be to get them from the interest groups that favor spending. For House members, it's every two years. Fund raising has to be in their minds constantly.

Campaign contributions do not buy spending programs outright, but they certainly load the dice in favor of a Congress that comes through with billions year after year. And for the donors, it will turn out to be one of their best investments.

The Committees

The system of assigning senators to committees also loads the dice for spending.

Senators from defense contracting states frequently go on the Armed Services Committee. First, because they request it. Second, because as I know from formerly serving on the Senate Democratic Steering Committee, which assigns Senators to committees, one of the most telling reasons for assigning senators to committees is the economic activity taking place in their states. "You can't leave Senator Grits off Armed Services! Do you realize the bases and the defense contract work in his state? He needs it for reelection."

This means, of course, that the Armed Services Committee, which is the Senate's principal adviser on military spending, will be loaded every year with senators who are enthusiastic about military spending.

On some committees there are surprising, even shocking, conflicts of interest, such as congressmen who own bank stock serving on the Banking Committee. But with disclosure now required of all owned capital by members of Congress, the conflict is probably limited. Disclosure helps greatly because it means that not only will constituents be more suspicious of a congressman's votes on issues related to his personal interests, but also his opponent at election time is now able to call vigorous attention to any abuse of power.

For many years the Energy and Natural Resources Committee

included only one member who came from a state east of the Mississippi. The result was that the Senate was sure to be confronted each year with proposals from that committee for multi-billion-dollar water projects. With that sort of committee momentum, it is almost impossible for any pro-economy platoon to slow down spending on a public works project, even if it is outrageously bad.

And so it goes. Senators who favor employment programs and more educational money apply for the Human Resources Committee and labor leaders often lobby to get them there; senators fascinated by transportation, who believe the country should make a much bigger investment in this area, usually get on the Commerce Committee. Senators who are being pushed by the big cities in their home states for reclamation and housing money fight to get on the Banking Committee and often make it.

President Woodrow Wilson called the committees "the little legislatures," pointing out that here is where most of the decisions of the Congress are made. It was true when he wrote it and it is still true now.

Mobilized Home Folks

Every senator must concern himself with two elements in his constituency. The first is the general opinion of the majority. The second, and more important for a senator interested strictly in survival, is the opinion of an intensely well-organized minority. For example, a majority of his voters may favor gun control. But if a minority opposes gun control so vehemently that it is the governing issue on how they vote, the "survival" position politically may well be opposition to gun control. The same principle holds for an issue like abortion, which can heat up a minority to the boiling point.

Spending occupies the same kind of position. Again and again I have surveyed my constituents—sending out 100,000 questionnaires and receiving a return usually exceeding 10,000. I ask them how they stand on spending, with respect to every major activity of the government. Again and again the replies have overwhelmingly opposed spending increases.

Wisconsin is a fairly typical state. The questions went to a geographic cross section of the population. A 10,000 response provides a reasonably accurate picture of public opinion. We consciously and carefully frame the questions to make them as neutral as possible.

The replies explicitly oppose more spending in every area of federal activity. They don't want the budget increased for education or health or defense; nor for space exploration, highways, environmental protection, nor for veterans, social security, nor for energy research. True, there is less opposition to spending for social security and education than for foreign aid and welfare. But the opposition is right across the board. There are no sacred cows, no exceptions. And I get thousands of letters, apart from the questionnaire replies, vehemently opposing excessive federal spending. Yet *most* of my mail is asking for increases in special programs.

"Do more for the farmers!" "Increase my veteran's pension!" "I can't live on my Social Security; I need more." "Support our elderly housing program in Racine. We have to have it!"

And when the home builders and unions and savings and loan associations want to turn on the mail with a letter-writing campaign, how they can do it! If there has ever been a home folks campaign to *stop* spending on a social service or defense program I haven't seen it—except when the environmentalists decide to try to stop a public works project. The environmentalists are usually outnumbered and outfinanced, but sometimes they win.

The Irresistible Claim

Almost all of us have had a dear relative or close friend who has suffered and died from cancer. And there's a fair chance, unfortunately, that you or I or anyone we know will be a next victim.

So let's spend whatever we can and beat it. Yes? The difficulty is that it takes something besides money—the open checkbook won't do it by itself for cancer any more than it has for education or better housing for the poor in our cities. But try to tell anyone in the Congress or the Executive that money isn't the answer. For as long as I can remember, President after President has come before us in the Senate calling for a more generous program to fight cancer. Congress responds in spades. Invariably there will be an amendment introduced to increase the budget above the President's request to fight cancer. Imagine you are a member of the Senate. Whatever you think about how much we may have wasted on the program, you start to visualize your opponent in the next election. "Don't vote for Simkins; he voted against cancer research. He's for cancer."

The result is that the National Institute for Cancer Research has been stuffed with more money than it can wisely use for years.

Donald Fredericksen, the head of the National Institutes of Health, has said that if he had another $50 million for the institutes, to spend wherever he wished, he would give none of it to cancer research. The reason is that competent research, and the coordination of all that research so that it can move in orderly and effective fashion toward overcoming cancer, is not simply a matter of mindlessly throwing every dollar we can beg or borrow into the fray. It's a matter of doing the hard, careful thinking, making the discriminating selection at the right time of the right personnel and the most useful research.

It is also a matter of saying no to some earnest, dedicated people. Which I did. And therein lies a little story I would like to tell as the conclusion of this chapter on how the spenders do it.

It is a story about a super-lobbyist and one of the most remarkable people in this country—a person I count as my valued friend —a wise and delightful lady, Ann Landers.

Her real name is Eppie Lederer and not long ago she was voted the most influential women in America. This story will bear that out. She should be influential. She's intelligent, compassionate, charming; she'd make an excellent President and a first-class senator.

I've known Eppie for more than twenty-five years. She came to Wisconsin long before she became a noted columnist. The first thing she did was take over the Democratic party in Eau Claire County, where, as in most county units, the party had been drifting along, electing no Democrats, its meetings attended only by a few members of the dominant local union, the Rubber Workers.

When Eppie hit town she went to one of these sleepy meetings with about twenty in attendance, no press coverage, and not much on the agenda except who was going to be the punching bag for the dominant Republican party to kick around in the next election. Eppie decided it was time for some action. She served notice on the startled union men at the meeting that they should get off their tails, pass out literature, knock on doors, raise money, sell memberships, tell the newspaper and radio stations the Democrats were in business, or get out and make way for someone who would do exactly that. The labor boys blinked, laughed, and adjourned to a nearby bar to talk about the five-foot-two dame with the big mouth.

So Eppie went to work. The next meeting was stacked with her friends. Labor got nervous and went to work too. At the next election of county officers, the city of Eau Claire had the biggest Democratic party meeting ever heard of. Instead of the twenty old standbys, six hundred brand new Eau Claire Democrats showed up, signed up, and elected Eppie's slate.

Eppie gets things done. She's charming, determined, and very bright. In 1978 she brought all her talents to bear in lobbying the Congress to spend more money on her favorite cause—cancer research.

In my years in the Senate I have been subjected to all kinds of lobbying entreaties. But this was something new and it was impressive.

On Sunday, May 7, 1978, a full-page ad appeared in the largest daily newspaper in my state, the *Milwaukee Journal.* The ad asked my constituents in Wisconsin to tell me to vote to increase the budget for cancer research by $158 million more than the President had requested.

The cost of that one ad to influence one senator to vote for one part of the appropriation bill, in just one of the Appropriations Committee's subcommittees, cost over $6000. It was paid for by a national organization with headquarters in New York City. I was singled out because I was a member of the subcommittee on appropriations for health, education, and welfare. Similar guns were aimed at other members of the subcommittee through expensive ads in local newspapers.

It was a great gambit. For if the subcommittee were to put the additional sum into the budget, it would be a very long shot indeed to try to take it out. As I have said, no politician wants to go on record as being anti–cancer research.

And that is why we have almost drowned the National Cancer Institute in federal dollars, under the misapprehension that if we come up with enough money we can prevent and cure the dread disease quickly. President Carter was not trying to hold down the cancer research budget because he does not want a cure for cancer. He recognized the fact—which most responsible experts at the National Cancer Institute will verify confidentially—that it takes time and brains and patience as well as money. The budget figure had already been increased from $178 million to $878 million in ten years, that is, by more than 390 percent. The House would go to about $900 million. The Ann Landers ads took it to $1036 million.

Here are excerpts from the ad that walloped me.

IF YOU WANT TO BE PART OF AN EFFORT THAT MIGHT SAVE MILLIONS OF LIVES—MAYBE YOUR OWN—PLEASE STAY WITH ME—Ann Landers

Dear Readers: For those of you who look to my column for laughs, sorry, I have nothing for you today. My message is a somber one, but it also offers you an opportunity to do something about the most feared disease known to man . . .

One out of every four Americans will get cancer at some time during his life. One out of every six will die from it, unless new treatments and cures are found. Scary, isn't it? Especially when you look at it this way: If you have a dinner party and invite five couples, two people at your party (including you and your spouse) may be a cancer fatality.

These are depressing figures, but the picture isn't all that black. Here are some encouraging signs:

We now know that there over 100 different types of cancer. We also know that 8 types of cancer, considered virtually hopeless ten years ago, have shown more than a 50% survival rate for five years or longer. Such spectacular progress is proof that medical research does pay off.

The more we hunt, the more we will find. Hunting costs money, but we must not let that stop us.

Medical research unlocked the secrets of T.B., diphtheria, small pox and polio. Medical research will eventually find cures for all cancers.

People complain about high taxes and government spending—and well they might. The cost of living is out of sight . . . Moreover, things will probably get worse before they get better.

The Federal Budget for 1979 is $502 billion, yes, I said Billions. That's a B. Is it unreasonable to ask Congress to spend an additional $158 million on basic cancer research, cancer centers, education of physicians in cancer treatment and prevention, and the development and use of new and improved drugs for clinical research? . . .

The Subcommittee on Appropriations for Health, Education and Welfare will very soon decide on whether or not our Government will spend the additional funds. Here is where you come in.

In your district, the key man is Senator William Proxmire. His address is Senate Office Building, Washington, D. C. 20510.

Write to your Congressman or clip this column . . .

After that ad appeared, I received over a thousand letters from constituents urging me to follow Ann Landers's plea to increase the appropriation for fighting cancer by $158 million more than

President Carter had requested. Other committee members were similarly implored by their constituents who had read local Ann Landers ads and responded.

When we met in subcommittee to discuss how much to put in the bill, the Ann Landers ad was obviously a potent, if silent, factor in our decision to increase the President's budget figure by $47 million ($25 million over the figure decided on by the House). The combination of a heart-wrenching appealing cause, big money (tens of thousands in advertising), and Eppie's machismo paid off.

Fighting shoulder to shoulder with her in this important cause is Mary Lasker, widow of one of the country's most brilliant advertising executives who was also a member of *Fortune*'s Business Hall of Fame. Together they are a mighty team. Mary Lasker is also attractive, persuasive, and a totally committed advocate of the government's all-out financial commitment to cancer research, which is why we have spent more than we should in response to an irresistible claim.

(9)

Two We Win
for the Taxpayer

IT CAN HAPPEN. The right sort of pressure from those who are sufficiently concerned, even outraged, can win a victory against great odds. This happened in our fight to stop the supersonic transport.

The Johnson Administration kicked off the battle for federal funding of the SST. The Nixon presidency threw its full force behind it. The program was at first a modest few million a year for research to develop a commercial plane that would fly at speeds of two to three times the speed of sound, or 1500 to 2000 miles per hour.

To be sure, the federal government has historically contributed mightily to the development of commercial aviation but always in the course of spending very large sums to develop military aircraft. The subsonic jets that gave this country its dominant lead in aircraft production grew largely out of our success with military jets.

The military has researched, developed, and produced tens of thousands of supersonic jets. There could be no objection to commercial airlines benefiting from this research and experience.

But the SST project was something different. It would have put the federal government into the commercial research business, eventually to spend as much as $5 billion to develop a strictly commercial transport. The principle was as wrong as it could be for many reasons, even excluding possible damage to the environment. First, the government should stay out of the free competitive market. It distorts the situation, since it can spend, with its huge resources and lack of concern for costs, far more than the market can or should support. Second, the proposal was not just to research the feasibility of a commercial SST —not just to develop it—but to make actual prototypes of a plane especially designed to benefit only the most affluent members of our population.

Here was a spending program, however, that seemed to have everything and everyone behind it. It had the President and his entire administrative entourage, including Defense, Treasury, NASA, and so forth. It had the powerful aerospace industry— especially the huge Boeing Company in Seattle, Washington, which would employ thousands of workers on the project, not only in Seattle but all over the country in fulfilling subcontracts. The AFL-CIO was pushing it—the Machinists Union has thousands of members in virtually every state. It had, too, the country's airlines' somewhat reluctant support, since they would be buying and flying the new queen of the skies.

And fortunately for Boeing, the funding was quarterbacked by two of the most respected and powerful members of the Senate, Warren Magnuson, then chairman of the Commerce Committee and a big wheel on the Appropriations Committee, and the other Washington senator, Henry Jackson, one of the most esteemed senate members on military and aviation matters.

In spite of all this artillery, they were beaten. At first there were only a dozen of us who would vote against the SST. Our little band included Senators William Fulbright and Robert Kennedy. We were small and weak and our defeats were embarrassingly complete.

But as the years went by, things began to turn around a little. The airlines began to sense the risk of spending so much for gigantic new planes that could burden them for years. Some of the most prominent newspapers in the country, among them the *New York Times* and the *Washington Post,* began to question the economics of a commercial plane that was designed to serve only the wealthiest of those who fly overseas and for whom there would be only a modest time saving—only a few hours—on trips to Europe or even to Asia. A few more senators began to come over to our side. Eminent economists like Arthur Okun and Walter Heller also helped by pointing out that the SST funding would be a misallocation of the nation's resources, as well as a weak prospect in commercial competition.

As late as 1969, however, I lost on an up-and-down vote when my amendment to stop the SST was beaten by a decisive 58 to 22 margin.

Then, in 1970, the troops of the environmentalists came on the field: the SST represented a threat to the environment. The result was one of the most dramatic turnarounds I have ever witnessed in the Senate.

As chairman of the Joint Economic Committee in 1970, I called hearings on the supersonic transport and asked the chairman of the President's Council on Environmental Quality, Russell Train, to testify. Train told the committee that a fleet of 600 SSTs flying regularly in the upper atmosphere could substantially increase the ultraviolet rays reaching the earth's surface.

Scientists argued that this higher level of radiation would inevitably increase the number of skin cancer cases in the United States. And another scientist, who had been adviser to Presidents Johnson and Nixon—both of whom supported the SST—told the committee that the sideline noise of the Boeing model of the SST would be "the equivalent of 50 subsonic jets taking off simultaneously." (This does not apply, of course, to the smaller, and slower, British-French Concorde.)

The upshot of the noise-impact problem was that anyone living within ten miles of an airport that permitted this particular SST to land would have to spend $6000 (that was a 1970 figure) to soundproof his home.

How could this be brought home to other members of Congress in a way that would convince them that the SST should not be produced until the radiation and noise problems were solved?

This is where the conservation and environmentalist organizations came in. They conducted a nationwide campaign, letting their members know about this new environmental threat and asking them to write their representatives and senators.

In the three weeks before the vote on the SST, I received more than 3100 pieces of correspondence on the SST from all over the country. More than 95 percent of it said the SST program should not get any more federal money. We checked with other Senate offices and found that our mail was typical.

What a magnificent lobbying job that was. On December 3, 1970, the Senate adopted the Proxmire amendment striking all funds for the SST from the Department of Transportation Appropriation bill. The vote: 52 to 41.

In a single year the Senate reversed itself on a spending issue against the combined influence of the AFL-CIO, the aerospace industry, and the President of the United States and his entire administration. The newspapers were a great help. But what really won the battle were the thousands of letters from concerned citizens.

The Concorde, by the way, has finally closed down. The British and French have agreed to stop all further funding and cut their losses at $2.5 billion. The program produced a pitiful seventeen planes. It was an economic disaster for England and France.

The Home Folks

All successes are not sweet. I am thinking of one of the most painful days in my life, when I had to go against my own constituents—not to speak of my own self-interest. But it is a story that is at the heart of our problem with runaway government spending.

On a beautiful Saturday morning I went out to La Farge in

western Wisconsin to tell the people in that little town, where the Kickapoo Dam had been scheduled to be built, that I would oppose the dam and ask the Senate to vote against it because I considered it a bad investment for the taxpayer.

I spoke outside a firehouse, to a hundred or so of the people who were directly affected by the dam project, which was to provide flood protection and recreational benefits to La Farge and other towns in the vicinity.

For about twenty minutes I explained why I thought the dam would cost more than it was worth. Then we went to it, with questions and answers that lasted for more than an hour and a half. At least forty to fifty opinions were voiced.

Not a single individual supported my position, nor could anyone understand it. Everyone wanted the dam built and they wanted the 1800-acre lake that would come with it. They spoke of the forty-year drive for the project, of the floods they had suffered, of the economic plight of this section of Wisconsin, of the long, hard struggle to earn a modest income, and of their hopes that the lake might mean a better economic future. One woman wept as she predicted that without the project she and her neighbors could not survive there any longer. A little girl also broke down in tears as she told me that fewer children in the district would mean the end of the school.

A number of men argued that the costs had increased because of the years of delay by the federal government and because of inflation. Why should they be penalized for this? One woman pointed out that the money poured out for a few hours of our presence in Vietnam would pay for the entire project even at the increased cost. A man asked how I could justify what the government was asking to spend in foreign military aid to both sides in the Middle East, when a small fraction of it would build the Kickapoo Dam.

Again and again they argued that the government had already spent $14 million, that the dam was 80 percent completed and should be finished. Actually, $10 million of that $14 million had been for land acquisition alone, and at least $46 million, probably much more, would have been required. The whole thing was a heartbreaking example of the overrun problem. The project was initially to cost $15.6 million in 1962. But by 1971 when, after much delay, the baseline was set, it had gone up to $24.53 million. Early in 1975 it was estimated at $38.48 million. By the time I spoke in La Farge, I had been told that the cost would be $51.55 million, a mammoth 112 percent overrun above the original baseline.

I knew that the cost would grow and grow before the project was finished and would not have been surprised to see it hit $100 million before we were through. To justify the project, the Corps of Engineers had increased their estimate for recreation benefits by more than 100 percent, which gave the project a hairline benefit-cost rationale. They could do this because the law permitted them to apply to this project a ridiculously outdated 3 1/8 percent discount factor—the usual sleight-of-hand mathematics. With a realistic discount factor, the costs would have exceeded benefits by more than two to one. (See Chapter 6.)

It was impossible to get this through to my La Farge constituents—that the cost to the federal government was not 3 1/8 percent but really more than 7 percent, and, at that rate, the project could not be justified even if all the already sunken-in costs, the $14 million spent, were written off. I knew that the expense of the dam would continue to grow—I had seen it happen hundreds of times—and then the American taxpayers would take a continually worse drubbing.

I had to oppose the project in spite of the rending pleas and arguments of people of my own state who had lived with this project and dreamed of it as their salvation for so many years. I asked the Senate to take it out of the public works bill.

The reaction in Kickapoo Valley has naturally been mostly boos, with a few quiet hurrahs whispered in my ear when I go back into the area. In fact, on one trip during floods in the area that occurred shortly after the project had been killed in the

Senate, the local sheriff felt it was necessary to see that I was escorted.

Around that time some of the La Farge citizens organized a mock funeral in effigy for me, in which a dummy labeled "Prox-mire" was paraded out from the town to the site of the dam and tossed with full ceremony into an empty area behind it. Some local residents refer to the dry, would-be but never-was body of water as "Lake Proxmire."

10

New York City—
How They Did It

NEW YORK CITY benefits from many of its citizens' talents, one of which approaches genius in extracting greenbacks from us when we visit that Baghdad-on-the-Hudson. New York has another distinction: it is the only city (or state for that matter) that has been bailed out of threatened default and possible bankruptcy by the federal government. Not once, but *twice.*

What makes this even more interesting is that New York is unquestionably the richest city in America, probably in the world. It is the financial capital of the world. It needs money as the Sahara needs sand or the oceans need salt.

The second bail-out, in 1978, was particularly astonishing. Here was a city whose eleven largest "clearinghouse" banks alone had more than $280 billion in assets. (Many other New York City financial institutions have additional tens of billions in assets.) Yet the city asked for, and got, a $1.65-billion long-term guarantee from Uncle Sam, while the banks sat on their hands and their huge resources.

A typical senator said to me: "I can't understand New York. If the biggest city in my state got into trouble, the bankers in that city would get together and provide a loan, with tough terms, requiring the city to cut spending and balance its budget. They would insist on the controls necessary to see that they would be paid back. But those huge New York City banks say they can do nothing to help their city."

The senator was right. Providing several times the amount of guarantees issued by the federal government over a four-year period to New York City would have been no hardship at all to those New York banks. They now have less than 1 percent of their assets tied up in loans to their own city. These banks lend more to shaky regimes in South America and Africa every month than they do to their own Manhattan, not to mention their loans to distant and risky real estate investment trusts.

But these bankers decided they'd rather try to knock down the federal government for a guarantee than risk their own capital for their own city.

And a federal government that had said no to Detroit in the thirties, when that city went bankrupt and paid its employees in scrip for eighteen months, and had let the whole state of Arkansas go bankrupt said, "Sure, take it," to New York City.

This is a dangerous precedent. One of the main factors that keeps our cities and states fiscally sound is the specter of bankruptcy and disgrace. Now that New York City has been helped—first with temporary loans in 1975 and then with a long-term loan guarantee in 1978—other cities will be encouraged to play fast and loose with their spending. Why shouldn't Uncle Sam help them, after helping the biggest and richest city in the nation?

Senators and congressmen were aware of this. They also knew that New York City banks had capital available. But they let the city have what it asked for anyway.

Consider, furthermore, that in the year when New York City got its federal $1.65-billion guarantee, the state of New York had enacted a $750-million tax cut—one of the biggest tax reductions in the country.

A state has the basic responsibility for its cities. Its sovereignty permits it to impose almost any restrictions or provide any assistance to them that it wishes. It can abolish or create cities, expand their jurisdictions or contract them. To be sure, the state's ability to act in this case was limited by the fact that New York City's budget is larger than New York State's budget—which is not the case anywhere else in the country. Still, the tax reduction—obviously very welcome and useful for all New Yorkers—suggests that the state might have done more for its metropolis.

There is also the fact that though New Yorkers cry loudly about all the taxes they pay without getting anything back, they had, in both 1977 and 1978, more direct federal grants per capita than any other big industrial state. Only five other states, and these with small populations and huge tracts of federally owned land, received a higher per-capita grant aid. These figures do not include expenditures for defense spending and dam construction. But they do include more than a hundred categories of direct aid: welfare, Medicaid, community development, education, public service jobs, and anti-poverty programs.

In spite of all this, despite Governor Carey's promise on TV's "Meet the Press" in 1975 that if the government provided temporary seasonal loans at that time, "New York will not be back," they did come back, three short years later.

Why did the federal government cave in and provide the $1.65 billion guarantee? There are lots of reasons.

New York, the National City

First, there's the tough political fact that New York represents a colossal bag of electoral votes in any presidential campaign. President Carter knew this and made his commitment during the 1976 campaign and repeated it later. President Ford may very well have lost the state through that one dramatic headline carried by the *New York Daily News* during the 1975 financial crisis: FORD TO CITY: DROP DEAD.

President Carter's support was helpful. But in this case it wasn't the decisive factor. What was more important was the feeling in the House and especially in the Senate that New York is a unique national city. In the House, the state's very large delegation of thirty-nine members, with several serving on the Banking Committee, did an extraordinarily effective job of persuasion. Western and Southern congressmen were reminded of the New York delegation's help on big public works projects in their states; midwesterners' memories were jogged about help on farm price supports.

Just as President Carter tended to make the New York rescue operation a Democratic issue, the Republicans, recognizing what had happened to President Ford, decided to make it their issue too. New York State legislators joined congressmen in pleading with fellow Republicans to keep the G.O.P. alive in the second biggest state. The New York bankers, strongly associated with both House and Senate banking committees, expertly lobbied those committee members to save the city as a matter of national interest.

It proved impossible to get strong witnesses ready and willing to come before our Banking Committee and give the "other side." Even though there were a number of thoughtful and influential members of the financial community, in New York and in other cities, who believed the long-term guarantees were not in the best interests of the country or even of New York City itself, none of them was willing to state their views publicly and run the risk of antagonizing the New York banks. I was told that if a Chicago banker or Wall Street financier were to appear as a witness opposing federal guarantees to New York, his institution would be in danger of exclusion from the deals floated by the big New York banks from then on. It is not surprising that they refused.

And then there was the run-for-President syndrome in the Senate. It's more than just a joke that in an election year you can say "Mr. President" in either the Republican or Democratic Senate cloakroom and half the senators in the room will turn around. I remember standing in the well of the Senate when the

New York City guarantee vote was being tallied. A fellow senator and I took turns, as the roll was called, at guessing how each
senator would vote. We hit it on the nose every time. Our guesses
were based not on ideology, but on which senators fantasized
about running for President and envisioned appealing for that
big, fat New York electoral prize.

New York—The World City

> Give me your tired, your poor,
> Your huddled masses yearning to be free,
> The wretched refuse of your teeming shore,
> Send these, the homeless, tempest-tossed to me:
> I lift my lamp beside the golden door.

Nothing expresses America at its generous best better than these
words of Emma Lazarus, inscribed on the Statue of Liberty in
New York Harbor. But they also express the city itself. They
may have been aimed at Europe; they could have been aimed at
the rest of America, for whom New York City is both a mecca
and the supreme challenge.

Congressmen, senators, and everyone in the country recog-
nizes that New York is still "where it's at," whether one wants
to get to the top in art, in business, on the stage, in writing, in
finance, clothes designing, music, ballet, or opera.

New York has six of the ten biggest banks in America, the
richest, and probably the brightest, law firms, six of the most
successful accounting firms, and the headquarters of all three of
the national TV networks. It's truly the Big Apple. If you want
to make it big, you don't go to Keokuk or Mobile; you tackle
New York City.

It has the newspaper that sets the world standard for excel-
lence in journalism. It has the most beautiful shops. It's the home
of the United Nations, which makes it as close to a world capital
as any city could get. It still has the most magical skyline in the
world.

The People

Some other cities have some of these elements. But what makes New York truly unique is its people. The taxi drivers somehow seem franker and more humorous. The waiters and the maître d's are more skilled at the friendly rip-off. The pace, the speech, the classic characters—can you imagine Damon Runyon, Billy Rose, Walter Winchell without a New York backdrop? Somehow Broadway Joe Namath has never been the same since he left the New York Jets. That New York backdrop is indeed essential.

And there's another New York City—aside and apart from Manhattan. I discovered it when I went to Brooklyn two days after Christmas in 1977 to work all day as a garbageman. As chairman of the Senate Banking Committee, I wanted to see what was going on. The prospect of further federal involvement in the city was coming up in 1978, when the seasonal loan program expired.

A major problem for New York, like other cities, is the cost of paying city workers—policemen, firemen, teachers, and so on. There are lots of ways of finding out how efficiently a city is being run. One can read newspaper articles and editorials, talk to the mayor and the aldermen, interview bankers, businessmen, and labor leaders. We had done all that. And our committee had held hearings to challenge New York City's fiscal operation.

It seemed time to get out and actually talk to the workers themselves, right on their jobs. There is just no substitute for spending a working day, side by side, sharing a job. After working together you have a chance to get frank, blunt viewpoints. And you get a feel of the job itself: its monotony and how tough it is physically. After a while your fellow worker relaxes and begins to tell you how he really feels.

The Brooklyn garbagemen worked hard. They were efficient. They used their trucks, sweepers, and incinerator aggressively. The truck we used, which had once turned over on the freeway, was eight years old. On another occasion its dashboard had caught fire. Any old key would start it. But it did the job.

There are some things New York City could do more efficiently with its garbage collection. A year before, I had spent a day with a Fond du Lac, Wisconsin, garbage crew. Officials had found a way to cut the work of garbage collection in half. Brooklyn could benefit from the Fond du Lac system, where private trash collectors use only two men on a truck, for instance. New York uses three.

The three men on my truck were friendly, helpful, and gave me an earful about New York City's problems. They worked hard and fast to keep warm. Several times they ran a few blocks to warm up. The people whose garbage was collected were also warm and friendly and since it was only two days after Christmas they even offered tips, which the crew invariably refused.

The whole experience gave me an entirely different view of the city and the kind of people who live there. I concluded from those days and later visits with firemen, policemen, hospital workers, and others, that the big labor cost for New York can be handled in a way that will permit the city to balance its budget.

The Brooklyn experience was useful in many ways. For one thing, judging by the attitude of the men, their pay seemed to be adequate, even after two years of holding raises down, and the city seemed in a strong position to continue to resist pay increases and to move toward a balanced budget.

I also realized a different dimension of New York City. The biggest illusion about it is that it begins and ends on Manhattan Island. Of course, that is the glamorous center of the city which visitors head for and often all that they see. But a good part of the population actually lives and works outside the island. Brooklyn is the most populous borough. And the most striking thing about people in Brooklyn, Queens, the Bronx, and Staten Island is that all in all they are not much different in their attitudes from people living in Oshkosh or Beaver Dam, Wisconsin.

It's the top brass in both city government and business in New York City that anyone about to lend money to the city has to worry about. New York officials are famous for suckering their natives, as well as us "peasants" from outside, into outrageous giveaways. (The Indians fell for it when they sold Manhattan for a few trinkets.) The performance of New York officials with regard to the Yankee Stadium gave New Yorkers as bum a deal as the original Indians got and was enough to create grave doubts in Washington about the feasibility of a long-term loan guarantee. This is how it went.

In 1977 the Yankees won the World Series and had a terrific year at the box office, grossing $9.3 million in admissions and $4.8 million from concessions. The city should have received nearly a million in rent. Instead, it took in less than $150,000, and the Yankees told the city they would cut the rent payment even lower.

A year before, in 1976, it was worse. The Yanks won the American League title and grossed more than $7 million. The city should have received more than $800,000 in rent. Instead, the city actually owed the Yankees $10,000. The joker here is the contract that permits the Yankees to charge off certain maintenance costs against rents.

This fatal contract also excluded the city from any participation in the most lucrative part of the Yankees' financial operations: TV revenue. On the surface it looks all right. The city gets a graduated percentage of the gross at the gate and a percentage, ranging from 5 to 10 percent of the take, from concessions. But with the fine print in the maintenance deductions clause, the contract becomes ridiculous, an almost transparent way for the Yankee owners to avoid paying any significant rent to a city which poured $100 million into renovating Yankee Stadium.

It is true that the million dollars or so a year the city lost on this deal wouldn't have balanced the budget. But if city officials permit knuckleheaded giveaways like this contract with an organization as visible as the Yankees, what faith could we have that it was conducting its business with its thousands of other contractors in such a way as to receive full value for the dollars it spends? Indeed it suggested that Congress would be doing neither New Yorkers nor taxpayers all over the country any favor by taking a soft attitude toward further federal assistance to the city.

It also suggested the city should take a long, hard look at sweetheart contracts.

Here is one of the most successful and the richest franchise in baseball, a sport as conspicuously covered by TV, radio, and newspapers as any activity inside the White House. We're dealing with a team that is argued about, deplored, and enjoyed in offices, factories, bars, kitchens, and living rooms not only in Harlem and Wall Street, Brooklyn and the Bronx, midtown, uptown, and downtown New York, but all over the nation. The imperial Yankees were the super team of the twenties, thirties, forties, and fifties. There was a popular book, later a film, entitled *The Year the Yankees Lost the Pennant,* so rarely did they not crush all opposition. And today they are once again dripping with success, not only with millionaire pitching aces and power-hitting outfielders, but with millionaire relievers and pinch hitters too.

What we saw in New York was the richest man in town robbing an orphan's piggy bank. To be a party, through condoning it, to New York's indulgent contract which made the Yankees richer still, so they could pay the huge salaries to take the best players away from other American cities, was something no red-blooded baseball fan from outside New York should ever permit.

The one saving grace was that the *New York Times* conspicuously, on a Sunday front page, reported this perverse contract and spelled out the details of the giveaway. And Harrison Goldin, the New York City comptroller, denounced it and called for renegotiation.

It is true that there were responsible people in New York protesting such sweetheart contracts. But the Yankee Stadium sting did take place, and New York back in the spring of 1978 was poised and ready to pass a much bigger sting on to the federal government. At least New York's top brass was.

Yet New Yorkers—most New Yorkers—are not that way at all. The letters I received from them when the federal government was deciding whether or not to give New York additional help to prevent the possibility of bankruptcy literally astounded me.

Because I was chairman of the Senate committee that would make the critical recommendation to the Senate, and because the New York papers focused some of their attention on my position on the issue, the mail from New Yorkers was heavy, day after day, for several months.

I would have expected—what with the press (New York), television, and radio supporting federal aid to New York, and with the mayor, governor, New York senators, and the whole New York delegation making federal assistance a holy crusade —to be deluged with mail asking me to ride to the city's rescue. Imagine my astonishment when consistently, three to one, letters said *don't*. New Yorkers wrote over and over again that if the Feds bailed out the locals, the locals would just continue their lazy, sloppy, sometimes wasteful, sometimes corrupt, and usually extravagant ways.

The New York mail was more consistently opposed to the federal bail-out than the mail from the rest of the country.

If you took it as a whole, the country seemed to oppose the aid to New York, but only by a two-to-one margin.

At that point a Harris poll, indicating general support nationally for federal assistance to New York, seemed to contradict my mail. But the poll was flawed by its approach.

All in all, do you favor the federal government guaranteeing loans to New York City if the City balances its budget and such a plan would not cost the taxpayers any actual money, or do you think it is better for New York City to default and go bankrupt?

In 1975 that might have been a reasonable question. In 1978, in my opinion, it was not. New York was not going to go bankrupt. It had made substantial progress, sharply cutting its rate of spending increases and moving vigorously toward balancing its budget. Jobs were increasing, unemployment dropping. Inflation was less than in the rest of the country. The banks were in far better shape to provide assistance, and to imagine that they would have permitted their city to go bankrupt with the consequences, especially the psychological ones for themselves, was absurd. A mere $2 billion or less for banks with a hundred times that much in assets. The Harris poll question was misleading.

A decision had to be made. Here was a precedent-breaking federal incursion into city fiscal policy, with all the dangers of other cities following suit and letting up on their responsibilities.

So, in January of 1978, I discussed the situation with other members of the Banking Committee, and in February we agreed unanimously on a report that recommended *no* additional federal financial assistance to New York City. This report found that there were sufficient resources available in New York City and New York State, from the various financial institutions and pension funds, to meet all of the city's financing needs.

The New York Powerhouse

It became a classic case. After our Banking Committee had made its *unanimous* decision—no fiscal help for New York City—that metropolitan city's forces went into action, and those of us who held out to the end never had a chance. We were, in effect, clobbered.

The first knight in armor was the *New York Times*. This paper's well-earned reputation for fairness and objectivity has given it an extraordinary credence among senators and congressmen, regardless of party or ideology. And the very fact that the *New York Times* is read so widely makes it a major means of communication in Congress.

How else do you think members of Congress find out what's going on? By listening to debates on the floor? If you have ever watched the House or Senate in session, you know that little attention is given to most debates. By reading the *Congressional Record?* The only senator I have ever known who read the *Record* faithfully was the remarkable Paul Douglas from Illinois, who would wake up at five every morning and read it cover to cover. Many "spot read" the *Record.* Most use it for occasional reference. As for committee reports, they also serve a usual reference purpose and can help in providing speech material. But they are not a major means of communication. And the informal, lunchtime, social conversation provides a useful exchange but without the coherence that the most complex issues require.

The one sure, consistent way members of Congress communicate with each other is through the press. The Washington papers play a big role, but the king of the press is the *New York Times.* A favorable editorial is manna from heaven. If a committee chairman can get a hearing covered by the *Times,* other members of Congress sit up and take notice. The paper's judgment and integrity are respected. Its news coverage is widely believed. It can support a bill and make it passable; its opposition can kill.

The *New York Times* covered its city's fiscal issue in Congress like a tent. It's no exaggeration to say that most congressmen saw the issue through the eyes of the *Times.* They believed its version of the problem. Our banking committee reports, our hearings, our debates on the floor were largely ignored by the press outside of New York City, so the *New York Times* version was the only game in town.

The *Times* was, as always, very fair, giving full play to all criticism of the proposed assistance. But the total picture for most readers was of a city struggling against odds to make the grade, and urgently needing a helping hand from Uncle Sam. This was the theme in editorials, in columns, and it had its effect not only on congressmen who had only a casual interest but also on members of our committee who were exposed to the hearings and the full process of committee debate. The *Times* wanted New York City to get that federal guarantee. The message was clear.

The other forces that turned the Senate Banking Committee from no in January of 1978 to yes in June were the New York senators. Jack Javits and Pat Moynihan did more to change the tune than any two senators I have ever seen operate on any issue in all my career.

It is rare that a senator will attend a hearing held by a committee of which he is not a member. Once in a great while, one may ask permission to move into alien committee ground and ask a question or two, or give a short speech in favor of his state's interest. But Javits and Moynihan, with complete deference and courtesy, simply moved in the wife and kids and camped with the Senate Banking Committee during the day-to-day, long hearings on New York City.

I was always there, because I was the chairman. Two or three members of the committee would attend at least part of most of the hearings. Others dropped in on a few of them, stayed for a half hour or so, asked a few questions, and left to attend other hearings. But Javits and Moynihan were present at virtually every minute of the hearings. They cross-examined every witness who appeared. Even the strongest witnesses for New York, like Mayor Koch and Governor Carey, had their best testimony greatly strengthened by the reinforcement of the two New York senators. Weaker witnesses were repeatedly saved by them. Opposition was up against the toughest kind of cross-examining techniques. Javits and Moynihan had done their homework, knew the issue thoroughly, and would let no generality or unsupported criticism of aid to New York go unchallenged.

Committee members were inevitably swayed by two of the

most intelligent and articulate men ever to serve in the senate. Jack Javits has had a lifetime of experience as an advocate—lawyer, state attorney general, congressman, and very effective senator. Pat Moynihan was a professor at Harvard, a mover and shaker in the administrations of four Presidents, one of the most colorful ambassadors to serve at the United Nations, and an imaginative, humorous, delightful persuader.

What was most impressive was that Javits and Moynihan cared enough about their city—they both grew up there—to devote such an enormous amount of time, coming to the hearings day after day, sitting at the end of the table because they were outranked by the committee members, and pleading so hard, with such verve, for their case. Any senator voting against New York aid had to feel he was letting down two colleagues who really cared. Senators like to accommodate each other on matters that deeply affect another's state, especially when the issue becomes emotional. We all have to live with each other, and to count on a degree of patience, forbearance, and tolerance from our colleagues when our personal convictions are at stake.

So, between the *New York Times* and Jack Javits and Pat Moynihan, our Banking Committee was turned around between January and June. Twelve senators changed their minds. Only Senators John Tower of Texas, Jake Garn of Utah, and I voted against providing New York City with assistance.

11

Why Bail Out Chrysler?

WHY SHOULD FEDERAL taxpayers bail out the Chrysler Corporation?

In just one year, 1978, more than six thousand American firms, large, small, and medium, went bankrupt. The federal government helped none of them. Most of them wouldn't have dreamed of asking. Some of the bankruptcies were caused by management incompetence. In some cases the public had just stopped using a product which had become as obsolete as the horse-drawn buggy. Sometimes the customers had moved from downtown into suburbs and the business had dried up. Or the vigor, push, and good luck of competitors had deprived the firm of its market.

In many cases a loan guarantee or a favorable loan would have saved the day. Why didn't the government step in, preserve the employees' jobs, and keep the business rolling?

In the past ten years Uncle Sam could have saved millions of jobs that way. It would have been a bonanza for the banks. Tens of thousands of businessmen would been spared the heartbreak of losing everything they had worked for. "Here it is," the government could have told them, "We won't let you fail." Maybe they needed only ten thousand dollars or a hundred thousand, or, as in the case of Chrysler, a billion and a half.

What's wrong with it?

Just about everything.

It's perfectly obvious that this kind of largesse would be the end of the free enterprise system. Millions of products and services with no real market would be produced by outmoded or inefficient firms. And the efficient, ongoing firms would suffer from unfair, government-subsidized competition.

One of the fixed tenets of the free enterprise system is that if you can't get it together—management, brains, a skilled work force, and the capital—and keep it together, you're out. That's it. The specter of failure is always over your shoulder; it keeps you alert and productive. Lenders and ownership investors in a business also know they are on their own. If they misjudge the value of their investment, they have to pay the price; if their judgment is good, they are rewarded. The system can be cruel, and it can throw innocent, hard-working men and women out of work, or ruin a conscientious person who has been unlucky or not quite competent enough. It can painfully hurt banks as well as owners.

But by and large the system works, and it works well. It reduces incompetence in management. It eliminates products when the demand for them has disappeared, whether they be gas-devouring automobiles or sailing schooners or women's bustles.

If government chooses unwisely to go down that long road of bailing out firms which have failed for lack of competence or judgment, the incompetence and lack of judgment remain; yet by one of the oldest laws of government spending, the bail-out must go on. Otherwise the stupidity and waste exercised by the government in the first place would be exposed. The bail-out has to be continued, even expanded.

Under such a policy you as a businessman would need neither competence nor back capital nor a product still in demand. All you would need to do would be yell for help. The government would take care of the rest.

That is why the government stayed out of the save-everybody business.

Until Lockheed. Until New York City.

When we bailed out Lockheed, and especially when that rescue worked without a government loss, we established a very, very dangerous precedent.

Lockheed was the nation's biggest defense contractor, and while the assistance went also to save a segment of the operation that was *not* defense and government procurement, the fact that two-thirds of Lockheed's production was military weaponry was the rationale for the bail-out.

In the case of Chrysler, there was no such excuse. To be sure, 5 percent of its production was tanks sold to the government, profitably for the corporation and to the satisfaction of the army. But this production would continue no matter what happened. Also, the Omni and Horizon compacts and the highly profitable operation in Mexico could and would be kept going in the event of bankruptcy. The justification for a bail-out was almost invisible.

*

Argument Number One. It was claimed that Chrysler, operating full blast, provided 119,500 direct jobs and 292,000 indirect ones (through dealers and suppliers) for a total of over 411,500. It was also claimed that in a worst-case situation, bankruptcy would trigger off the temporary loss of 500,000 jobs and a permanent loss of about 200,000. This was patently ridiculous. No other bankruptcy has ever resulted in such a loss of jobs and this one certainly would not.

Bankruptcy simply gives a company a breathing spell. New management may be required. Stockholders may suffer a loss and several years without dividends. Creditors have to stand back and wait, and probably lose some fraction of their loans and the accumulated interest.

Certainly some jobs are lost. But a great many are not. If the product is viable, the work resumes after the company has peeled off its high cost, perhaps by closing units. In Chrysler's case, plants employing thousands of workers would have had to be shut down in any event. The difference in number of jobs lost between a Chrysler bailed out by the federal government and a Chrysler in default and operating under a court reorganization procedure might be relatively small.

*

Argument Number Two. Chrysler should be saved because the automobile business needs three big competitors, not two. The argument is that a big three is oligopolistic enough to preserve a free market in which the price is not the result of a conspiracy. But even with three firms this may not be true. One firm will lead —the other two follow. Performance and style, rather than price, are often the prime competitive elements.

Of course, competition is significantly better with three instead of two firms. But with foreign competition providing the principal performance as well as the price options for American customers, the actual benefits of a weak competitor to Ford and General Motors are probably quite modest.

But there's a much more important consideration here. What kind of competition do we really have when one of the three competing firms has the government and its endless resources as its principal creditor? Certainly the terms recommended by the Treasury and accepted by Congress would not *at first* give Chrysler an unfair capital advantage. But that's only the first round. As Chrysler needs more and more, the government puts in more and more. This enables Chrysler to keep trying performance and engineering and style innovations until it hits the jackpot. Meanwhile Ford gets in trouble. Having helped out a competitor, what can the federal government do except help Ford?

Which puts the federal government up to its neck as a creditor of two of the big-three producers in an industry which has above all others been recognized as the flower of American free enterprise.

*

Argument Number Three. Chrysler's plight was not its own fault. It was the result of federal environmental and miles-per-gallon requirements. Ford and GM, with their far larger size, were able to meet these more easily because they had the capital for costly research and development that Chrysler could not afford.

There's something to this; government regulations may well have had a different and discriminatory effect on the three competitors. But this was taken care of last fall: Chrysler won the advantage of using the GM emission technology. Environmental compliance may or may not have cost them more per car than it did GM, but the difference certainly cannot be called a major reason for Chrysler's problems. (More important causes are a series of bad management decisions: immediately after the Arab embargo, the company failed to go with smaller, more fuel-efficient cars and stuck with the larger automobiles; it purged engineers and designers to reduce cost and overhead, although strong engineering had been Chrysler's prime strength; and during the past decade, it made heavy and poorly timed investments in European facilities in order to compete with the international growth of Ford and General Motors.) In any event, no one has seriously suggested that the Government should resolve the inequality among American companies by paying the difference in cost to outfits bearing a higher relative burden. It would require billions upon billions of dollars a year.

On the miles-per-gallon requirement, Chrysler insisted it had been unfairly hurt by the government. But at the same time it declared that its Omni and Horizon cars and its very profitable investment in Japanese production had given it a miles-per-gallon advantage that would make it worth the government's while and pocketbook if they helped Chrysler out. Not only would it meet the miles-per-gallon requirements but, more important, make Chrysler a winner in the next few years over all its competition. Chrysler could hardly have it two ways. On one side of its mouth it was saying that government requirements had put it behind the eight ball. On the other, it was arguing that its little light cars would beat the opposition in the near future.

And nowhere, never did Chrysler tell us what the cost of installing the new emission technology had been. No figures on the cost in each year—1975 through 1978—nor on how they compared with Ford's and GM's costs. If Chrysler had a case there, they would have told us to the penny. The most serious rebuttal of the Chrysler position that government regulations caused their difficulties comes from the Highway Safety Division of the Transportation Department. After a one year study, using the automobile company's own factual data, the Division concluded that the smaller firms actually have a lower—not a higher —a lower cost than the larger firms. The Division calculated this on the cost per car. It examined the companies' own data and found that Chrysler spent less than Ford on a per vehicle basis, both in research and development and in investment to comply with federal regulations.

The Division released its study in the middle of our mark-up session. The Administration was distressed. Chrysler's bail-out supporters on the Committee huffed and puffed about the Division having a stake in defending its regulations. But there was no disputing the fact that this was the only study that had examined the industry's own data critically and analytically.

The study knocked out the argument: "The Government got us into this mess, it should bail us out of it."

*

Argument Number Four. If Chrysler should go bankrupt, the overall effect on the economy would be bad. Recession would be deepened and perhaps lengthened. This argument wholly overlooked the effect of a bankruptcy proceeding. It could not under any conceivable circumstance simply shut down that massive conglomerate corporation. Most of it would continue to operate, with most workers still coming to work every day. Cars would be produced and dealers would go on selling them. Suppliers would go right on supplying necessary parts. The firm might be smaller if certain segments were lopped off. That could mean jobs lost, but the jobs involved in producing gas-guzzling or luxury cars that were unprofitable couldn't last anyway without eternal government subsidy.

As for the anti-inflation effect of competition, certainly a reorganized company with its excess baggage peeled off could offer better, tougher, stronger, and more enduring competition than the same old management limping along with a government crutch.

That's why I vote against bailing out Chrysler. The decision would be a real watershed for American business, for our economy, and for our taxpayers. A bail-out would be a signal for corporations to line up—big, medium, or small. Who's next? It wouldn't be necessary to be a city like New York or a utility like Penn Central or the country's major defense contractor like Lockheed. Anybody would be welcome. And we could make a far stronger case for the five million firms that are smaller than Chrysler.

If taxpayers had thought before 1979 they were being had by their government, here was a whole new explosion of spending, in a brand new dimension.

The saddest thing about such a situation is the gross inequity of the contest in Congress. Chrysler hired two of the top lobbying firms in Washington—one Democrat, one Republican—the best money can buy, lobbyists who know how to appeal to both liberals and conservatives, and who were willing to work day and night on the bail-out.

There were no lobbyists working against the bail-out.

Chrysler couldn't lose. All the power, the clout, the money, the influence were on one side: the President and his entire executive branch—Treasury, Commerce, Budget, Labor, Defense, the works. Then there were the United Automobile Workers with hundreds of thousands of members all over the country. The UAW is highly respected; it is clean; it is honest; its leadership is highly competent. It is generally a solid public-interest-oriented force. So when it goes for a special payoff it carries one whale of a wallop.

Then the banks. Chrysler was into the banks for billions of dollars. If it went bankrupt, there would be not only embarrassment but, in some cases, significant losses, at least temporarily. I am not talking about a few Wall Street banks, nor those confined to the six states where Chrysler has its most concentrated production, but banks throughout the country. And, as we have seen, banks and bankers are uniquely effective in influencing members of Congress. They are community leaders, contributors or lenders to election campaigns. When they speak out, they are listened to.

Last, but not least, came the Chrysler workers and suppliers themselves. In six states, and with twelve senators, they could command an imposing vote. Letters, phone calls, and visits can make it clear what the crucial vote is for them, their families, and their relatives. The suppliers alone employ hundreds of thousands in many more than the six states. The dealers too: I doubt if there is more than a handful of congressional districts, and certainly no states, that do not have a Chrysler dealer. Usually there are scores of them and they can't be expected to be silent when their livelihood is threatened.

The bail-out army was impressive. Who was on the other side, protesting that the taxpayer should not be called upon to bear a loss or risk of loss that stockholders and banks are precisely rewarded for bearing? Who was ready to say that this was a precedent that could haunt our system for years to come?

The answer: virtually no one. Oh, there was some excellent editorial protest. The National Association of Manufacturers (NAM), an organization I do not always find in my corner, indicated that it disapproved of special government financial assistance for Chrysler, though it was not likely that the NAM would mount a major lobbying campaign on the issue. In fact, all the power, all the money, all the skilled lobbyists, all the labor clout and business clout and banking clout, plus the force of hundreds of thousands of Americans who had an immediate stake in the decision, were on one side.

The Chrysler bail-out couldn't lose. But the American taxpayer did—and will.

12

It's Not All Bleak

"PROXMIRE," said an Appleton, Wisconsin, man to me one night at a Chamber of Commerce meeting, "if things are so bad in Washington, you must be part of the problem. You've been there quite a while. Your speech and your answers indicate there's nothing good about the way the government is operating and plenty that's wrong. Isn't there anything they've done right since you became a senator?"

By the time my plane landed in Washington, I had been doing some thinking and decided the Appleton questioner had an excellent point. So the next day I told some of my staff I was going to give a series of speeches on the floor of the senate on what's right about a lot of our federal spending. At first they couldn't believe me. "No one ever finds anything right about the government. Even the pro-spenders. It's kind of unpatriotic." Another protested by quoting a remark of Will Rogers which demonstrated the folklore that no floor speeches would overcome: "This country has come to feel the same when Congress is in session as when the baby comes up with a hammer."

The most cynical response was that I wouldn't find enough to say for a five-minute speech.

How wrong that turned out to be. Over the next several months I delivered twenty-three speeches on what's right with the federal government.

Actually it is doing many things well, and continues to improve in a great variety of ways. For the purposes of this book we can by-pass the excellent progress in promoting civil rights and women's rights and rights of the poor and in other areas not primarily related to spending.

Starting with *health,* though Medicare and Medicaid have contributed to inflation, these programs with all their faults have made this a sounder, more just, and more compassionate country. The incomes of retired persons are greatly reduced. Medicare pays doctor and hospital bills and is responsible in large part, since it became law, for a remarkable increase of some two years in longevity among the population. It has also saved hundreds of thousands of ailing elderly from exhausting their last material resources, perhaps selling their homes, to pay for medical care they couldn't otherwise afford.

Medicaid has similarly helped the poverty-stricken of all ages to survive. Medical care is now so expensive that in many cases the poor would literally die without the Medicaid program.

Health research has cost billions and the bills go up every year. But it has indeed sharply reduced the incidence of heart disease and has made some progress in curing cancer, not to speak of a myriad of other diseases that have been slowed down or eradicated.

With *Social Security* we reap the most durable and defensible fruits of Franklin D. Roosevelt's New Deal. Though it is now the most costly government program we have, its principle is absolutely right. In an industrial society, even the most prudent wage earner can have his savings wiped out by layoffs, inflation, accident, or lasting illness. Social Security is based on the sound notion that the worker can earn his retirement pension, pay for it himself, and enjoy the dignity of living on it without welfare or poor-farm charity when he retires.

Of course any program that pays benefits to more than thirty million citizens, almost all of them voters, is subject to serious abuse. For years the Congress increased the benefits in every election year by amounts far exceeding increases in the cost of living. But now Social Security benefits are indexed to the cost of living as they should be. Any increases will have to wait for a rise in real wages (allowing fully for inflation) of the workers whose earnings provide the financial basis of these benefits. In the past ten years real weekly earnings have actually declined.

Earlier in this book I was very critical of *military* waste. In fairness, it must be said that our military has, with all its faults and indulgences, kept us well ahead of our major adversary in the world—the USSR. For many years I have chaired annual hearings of the Joint Economic Committee's subcommittee to receive testimony, from both the CIA and the Defense Intelligence Agency, comparing the economy and the military strength of this country and the Soviet Union. Such hearings have consistently disclosed that Russia spends more money than we do on defense. They have about twice as many military personnel. Yet in almost every aspect of military technology we have consistently maintained the lead. They have more submarines. Ours are faster, more reliable, quieter. Their missiles have a bigger megatonnage. But we have far more warheads (nuclear explosives) and our missiles are more accurate, more thoroughly tested. In some cases the quantity of their armaments is greater —tanks, for example. But with regard to every item the quality of our weaponry is ahead.

It is said that since World War II there has been a technological revolution about every five years. In any contest for military parity or supremacy, technology is the name of the game. Staying on top and ahead is not easy and it's not cheap. Our military has succeeded in doing that and deserves full credit for it.

Environmental protection— how fast this has come on us as an essential! In the 1968 presidential election it was considered so secondary in importance that not a single presidential or vice-presidential speech was devoted to the subject.

Now that we have discovered, and discover more each month, what ravages have been visited upon our earth, water, and air, we have awakened. Friends of the Earth, the Sierra Club, and other organizations have done a remarkable job of stirring us to action. It's a multibillion cost to government. The cost to private industry is even greater.

There are protests about this. Inflation is said to have increased by at least half a percentage point just because of environmental protection requirements. Actually this is an illusion, and one based on a fundamental irony: water and air are treated as free goods and are assigned no commercial value, though they are absolute necessities. They are not, traditionally, considered a part of the Gross National Product, so that cleaning up the air and water is considered a *cost* but not a usable product. Cleaner, fresher air is deemed to be worth nothing. Cigarettes have a multibillion-dollar value. Obviously the statistic showing that environmental protection is inflationary is a real phony.

But count our blessings. The pollution of our environment is now engaging our government, thanks to the terrifying facts that have been realized at last. The year 1977 marked the first year in our history when the air was cleaner than it had been the year before. This is a great federal contribution, one for which future generations may thank us.

The case for *consumer protection* is not as clear cut. Some of the consumer legislation has been badly conceived and miserably administered. I was the author of the Truth in Lending Law. It took us eight long years to win congressional acceptance of it; we were up against the powerful banking fraternity and many other business groups. What I had in mind was a simple disclosure statute. In our hearings we had exposed the rip-offs: 50 percent and 100 percent annual interest rates charged by some merchants, and the ignorance of some consumers, no matter how well educated, about how badly they were being chiseled by high interest rates. Say a woman bought a secondhand sofa for $50. The terms were $10 down, $5 a week, which would include 200 percent interest for many, many weeks. It would not be rare for the woman to pay from $100 to $200 in interest for that $50 sofa before she was through.

But the Federal Reserve Board drafted regulations so complex that it took the lender hours to fill out the form, and the borrower got lost trying to read it. A simple five words—True Annual Rate____; Finance Charge____ —were all that was needed.

A simplification bill has now been ratified by the Senate.

Truth in Lending has on the whole been constructive. A recent study by the Federal Reserve shows that since the law was enacted most consumers, including the poor, have begun to understand the intricacies of interest charges and are able to shop for credit.

Fair Credit Reporting, Truth in Advertising, Food and Drug Administration regulations have all helped in some measure to protect consumers and promote a more honest relationship between buyer and seller.

For many years economists flatly maintained that government efficiency never improves and there can be no increase in federal productivity. Since productivity is simply a measure of how much output each unit of input achieves, this was a ridiculous assumption. But it lies behind many statistics of the government itself. The assumption has been expensive, because increased efficiency would have been a great way to cut government costs and government spending without reducing government services. "There can be and will be no increase in government productivity" became a self-fulfilling prophecy. If government workers are not expected to improve their output, there will be little demand or likelihood that they will.

Fortunately the government has recently had some pioneers and heroes in this area. Back in 1962 Kermit Gordon, President Kennedy's chief of the Budget Bureau, published a study called "Increasing Government Productivity." It was an eye opener. It studied output per hour of government employees, showing small improvements in some agencies, spectacular improvement in others. The fact that some agencies were doing so well suggested that there were areas where costs could and should be cut. Strangely, there was relatively little interest in Congress or the

Administration in this promising opportunity to hold down government spending.

Elmer Staats, who is the Comptroller General and, as such, head of the General Accounting Office, comes as close to being the nation's guardian over spending as you can find. He has pushed hard to interest the Congress and the White House in a drive to increase government productivity. He has had some success, but even with an engineer-manager type of President like Jimmy Carter, his ideas are barely visible.

Tom Morris has been tireless in his fight to hold down spending in the Departments of Defense and of Health, Education, and Welfare. He and Staats and others have succeeded in persuading most of the government agencies to take the first big step in systematically making the federal government more efficient instead of just talking about it.

That first step is *measuring* productivity, just as businessmen do in the private sector. Staats and Morris have made surprising progress in making agency managers aware of how well or poorly they are doing. More than half of all government work is now measured for productivity improvement, and, in a study of forty-five major agencies, it was found that in recent years the increase had approached 2 percent each year. That's encouraging, indicating as it does that at any rate the taxpayer is getting a little more for his money. Even a fractional improvement (in the private sector it has averaged about 3 percent throughout the years) could save literally billions.

The sharp difference in the performance of different agencies was pointed out in a study done by Thomas Rosen of the Civil Service Commission and Thomas Morris, the then assistant director of the Office of Management and Budget. One hundred eighty-seven organizations within forty-eight agencies were studied. Of these, fifty-eight had a decline; but seventy showed a rather spectacular 4 percent improvement over a five-year period.

The reason seemed quite clear: the more productive agencies

had been more ready to install manpower-saving equipment. When computers do the work of a score of clerks, the output goes up sharply. One dry, matter-of-fact report from an army organization stated: "An automatic nailing machine costing $38,185 saved 20 men in constructing pallets for bombs. The annual savings of $240,000 resulted in an amortization period of 57 days."

The machine paid for itself in less than two months. And, in five years, the machine actually saved the taxpayer a beautiful $1.25 million—at a cost of less than $40,000. In another case, a labor-saving expenditure of $50,000 was paid back in forty-one days, earning $300,000 for the taxpayer in the first year. So, by five years, the original investment of $50,000 had earned $1.5 million.

These army successes (the majority of their labor-saving devices paid for themselves in less than 180 days) show the opportunities the government has, but does not use, to cut costs. The trouble is that, unlike any well-run business in the private sector, the government lacks the incentive to do it. In fact the incentives all point the other way.

After all, what happens when the manager of a government agency introduces a manpower-saving machine? First, those who were doing the job in the old, less efficient way lose their jobs. Eliminating jobs is not the best way to win a popularity contest in the government. Second, the importance of an agency manager is often measured by the number of people he commands and the size of his budget.

Staats and Morris, with their efficiency pleas, face a stormy future in government. Progress is slow, but it is coming modestly and quietly. Their effort deserves great credit. It is progress merely to have some of us on the Appropriations Committee now ask agency heads, who come before us for budget approval, to tell us what steps they are taking to measure productivity and what these measurements show. Their answers provide a solid basis for congressional approval or criticism of their budgets.

What would you consider the principal economic advantage this country has over the Soviet Union? Factory productivity? Retail distribution? Transportation systems? Lower cost and higher quality communication systems? It's true we're ahead in all those respects. But the major advantage we have over Russia is in *agriculture*. It's not even a contest, we're so far ahead.

More than 30 percent of all Russians work at farming, compared to 3 percent of Americans. With a larger population than ours, they have ten times as many farmers per capita, yet we produce 20 percent more food. We do this through farmers who in many cases hold other jobs on the side. In Wisconsin, for instance, where our dairy farming is the most productive in the world, we produce 38 percent of America's cheese with less than 2 percent of the population. About half of our dairy farmers have full-time jobs off the farm. And since manpower is still the number-one economic resource, the freeing of it from farming, made possible by agricultural efficiency, is a prime reason for our general production advantage over the USSR.

How do we do it? The heart of the advantage is the family farm. The farmer owns his own land, his herd, his equipment. He is in competition, with most of his crops, with thousands of other farmers. Fertility of soil and productivity of his herd and his amount of capital equipment may vary, but by and large his success or failure depends on his own efforts—or, I should say, the efforts of him and his whole family.

Incentive and motivation give American agriculture its advantage. This point is dramatized by the often-noted difference in Russia between the productivity of the small, privately owned gardens and that of the massive collective farms.

Much credit for our productivity should also go to the United States Department of Agriculture. I've given them more than one Golden Fleece—there's time-serving and there's waste—but over the years they have done a sensational job in improving the efficiency of the American farmer.

Year after year the number of farmers declines, and yet their production goes up. The county agent system has given farmers throughout the land technical assistance in management of land, herds, and equipment. Know-how is shared and promoted vigorously. Virtually every farmer is less than an hour's drive from a county agent. Soil conservation services of the department have greatly magnified the fertility and production of our farms. Research services have made sensational breakthroughs in making farm animals and equipment more productive. Agricultural credit through the Farmers Home Administration and Production Marketing Agency has helped farmers with the capital they need. In spite of its sometimes high cost, the system of supports, surplus storage, and promotion practices such as food for peace and food stamps have provided the expanding market and more stable income that have enabled hundreds of thousands of efficient farmers to stay in business and eventually prosper.

It's hard to believe, but it is true, that even with painful inflation American food is still a great bargain. Americans now pay less of a percentage of their income for food than they have ever paid before. We pay 17 percent of our income, and the percentage has fallen in every decade for many years. We also pay less, far less than residents of any foreign country anywhere else in the world.

Our federal government, through the good auspices of the Department of Agriculture, deserves a major share of the credit.

Indeed we are wasting money when *unemployment compensation* is abused. It should be improved and made more responsible. But without doubt it's essential and, like Social Security, is one of the great reforms of the New Deal that has kept this country out of another Great Depression.

Without unemployment compensation, a layoff can be a miserable catastrophe for a worker and his family. How can he keep up payments on house, car, life insurance, and still eat, if his income completely disappears? And as often happens when hundreds are laid off in the same community, there may not be any jobs available for weeks, even many months. What should the family do? Bow their heads and seek welfare?

Before unemployment insurance was enacted, our country suffered regular, deep, paralyzing depressions, with as much as 15 percent to 25 percent of the work force unemployed and without funds. Business bankruptcies increased the dislocation of the economy and the nation was on the verge of a catastrophe of the first order. Unemployment compensation puts a cork in the bottle before it can explode. The price is high, but it's worth it.

*

Two agencies that in the past received my Fleece of the Month Award have also been given Awards of Merit for wise, economical and effective use of the taxpayers' money. One went to the Smithsonian for building its Air and Space Museum on time, for less money than was originally requested, and for an improvement rather than reduction in its quality. I cannot find another example of a building, weapons system, or water project where this has been the case.

The museum opened on July 1, 1976—four days early. It cost $500,000 less than it was projected to cost ten years earlier in 1966. And it included at least four major features not projected in the original plans: a large theater, a planetarium, an art gallery, and facilities for handicapped visitors.

The second award went to the National Science Foundation, which I had strongly criticized in the past for frivolous or ridiculous projects. Three of its major activities deserve praise and acclaim.

1. The NSF funded work to build a man-made working gene, the basic chemical unit which, in combination, controls the growth and development of all living things. This breakthrough was heralded around the world and may well pave the way for producing large quantities of hitherto expensive, rare, and medically important substances such as insulin and infection-fighting chemicals.

2. Research sponsored by the NSF achieved promising results in finding methods of improving on nature's way of replenishing nitrogen in the soil. One method increases the number of edible plants that can interact with bacteria living at the plants' roots, in order to "fix" atmospheric nitrogen in the earth. The other is an exotic approach that involves getting the plants themselves to fix the atmospheric nitrogen without the presence of bacteria.

With a serious energy crisis upon us, these breakthroughs might be developed to substitute for artificial chemical fertilizers, which cost U.S. producers over $2 billion last year.

3. The National Science Foundation funded supporting research on how the brain recovers after being damaged. For the first time biologists can study how nerve growth takes place in a particular part of an injured brain. This type of basic research should promote a clearer understanding and better treatment of a whole range of nerve-related medical problems.

I gave a third Award of Merit to the Farmers Home Administration (FHA) for its remarkable job of increasing the productivity of its programs. In the period 1972–1976, the FHA had a 32 percent increase in the weighted total of the loans it made and serviced; at the same time it reduced the number of its employees by 3 percent. Some 265 fewer persons serviced over 2000 additional farm-ownership, low-income housing loans, and community loans for watersheds and sewers, among the nineteen major programs included in their productivity index.

This was achieved through the governmentwide productivity program sponsored by the General Accounting Office, using the same kind of measurement system that is widely used in the private sector. It has been found, and I would like to emphasize, that many aspects of government can be automated (sending out Social Security or Veterans' Administration checks, for example), at a saving of tens of millions of dollars.

A very special award of merit should go to the man who was conspicuously entitled to a limousine to take him back and forth to his job as head of the Veterans' Administration and refused it. That man is Max Cleland, who, in spite of the fact that he is a triple amputee, drives himself to his office in his own car. Cleland lost both legs and an arm when he deliberately fell on an exploding grenade in Vietnam to save his companions.

Time and again, before our Appropriations Committee, I have found it harder to part government officials from their limousines —those gas-guzzling, dollar-swallowing ego boosters—than from pet budget proposals providing their agencies billions. As I have said, there are a great many federal employees who insist on this symbol of class and distinction although the law makes it clear that only cabinet officers, the President, the Vice President, the Chief Justice, and a very few others are entitled to the $16,000-a-year privilege over and above their salaries.

If Max Cleland, who carries the burden of a $20 billion budget, supervises 200,000 employees, runs the biggest medical and adult education programs in the country, and one of the biggest insurance programs, can drive himself to work in his own seven-year-old Oldsmobile, specially equipped for a driver with one arm and no legs, why can't commission chairmen, undersecretaries, administrators, generals, and admirals do the same?

It must be said that Cleland's example has done more to eliminate the limousine-and-chauffeur self-indulgence than any other action I know. There has been an appreciable cutback in the number of long, black cars on the avenues of Washington.

13

What to Do About It

PART I: THE BUDGET

WHAT SHOULD BE DONE to end huge federal deficits, balance the budget, and bring government spending under control?

First, we need to realize that although we've tried to do these things in the past, we haven't succeeded. Presidential promises of a balanced budget haven't been kept. And countless congressional campaigns squarely based on, "Elect me and I'll fight to hold down spending," have merely given the nation Congresses that continue on the big spending path.

There are a number of proposals, including a constitutional amendment, to deal with this. At the beginning of the 1979 session of Congress, I introduced a bill that has the support of fifteen senators, varying from the most conservative to the most liberal, as cosponsors.

This bill would ensure that each year Congress submit a budget that would be in surplus if the economy grows in real terms —that is, allowing in full for inflation—by 3 percent or more. If growth is less than that, the budget would automatically be in deficit.

Consider how well the nation would have been served by such a system if it had been in effect during the seventeen years leading up to 1979. During those seventeen years, the budget was in deficit sixteen times—some years very big deficits—and in balance only once, with a small surplus. As a result, the country amassed a mammoth deficit during a period of strong economic expansion, which now requires the budget of 1980 to provide for interest payments on a national debt of about $58 billion.

Much of the current inflation is the product of these continuous, year-after-year deficits.

Now assume that the Proxmire bill had been in effect during this seventeen-year period. Instead of sixteen deficits and one small surplus, there would have been twelve surpluses and five deficits. Instead of suffering the huge increase in the national debt that has come to plague us in full force, we would have had a sharp reduction in the national debt. There would have been fewer inflationary pressures caused by the government. Interest rates would have been lower, and the combination of lower interest rates on the national debt, along with a smaller debt, would have brought the interest cost down to $20 billion or less —a reduction of $38 billion in what the government has to spend on the national debt. If my bill had been in effect during this seventeen-year period, we would have been able to balance the budget in 1979 with no changes in spending or revenue.

You may say, Why not simply require that the budget be balanced each year and be done with it? Why all the hocus pocus about a 3 percent growth in the national economy? The answer is that attempts to balance the budget in periods of slow growth and especially in periods of recession would be counterproductive. Can you imagine trying to balance it between 1930 and 1940? In that kind of depression, even refusing to fund essential government obligations would not have balanced the budget. Such drastic action would simply have aggravated the financial crisis. And any further taxes would have made the business situation even worse.

The blunt fact is that in periods of slow growth or recession, we need a deficit to stimulate the economy. At other points in the business cycle, we need to restrain inflation by keeping expenditures below revenues. The Proxmire proposal would do exactly that. It would provide a surplus in periods of above-average growth, and a strong surplus in periods of exuberant growth and inflationary pressure.

The distinguished economist, Dr. Paul McCracken of the University of Michigan, who has also served as a highly competent chairman of the Council of Economic Advisers, has written me supporting my proposal and calling it the most reasonable budget-balancing solution he has seen.

Some other economists have been critical, arguing that the stimulus needed from the government during recoveries from recessions would be too limited. They feel it may be necessary to come out of recessions with vigorous government spending and reduced federal taxes in order to establish a strong growth momentum.

That is precisely what has been wrong in the past. We have tried to emerge from recessions like Marines swarming to the rescue, throwing in every kind of spending program to put the unemployed back to work. For instance, in coming out of the relatively slight recession of the early sixties, the Kennedy Administration advocated an expansion of public works spending. Congress acted, but by the time the program could get well under way in 1967 and 1968, the economy was beginning to overheat with the Vietnam War. The program turned out to be inflationary as well as deficit-producing at exactly the time we should have been running budget surpluses to soak up the distending effect of military spending.

One of the crucial problems is the full-employment dream of many of our economists. They feel that the government should consistently set full employment as a theoretical goal. The Humphrey-Hawkins law now sets the goal at 4 percent unemployment. That was the level the nation reached, for the last time, in the sixties, just before we took off into the long inflation nightmare. And even during those boom years the budget was, with a single small exception, continuously in deficit—big deficit.

The Proxmire balanced-budget proposal has two escape

valves. First, the Congress could vote to set it aside at any time. Second, it is a law, not a constitutional amendment. It can be changed, modified, or amended by a simple majority vote of both houses of the Congress, subject of course to presidential veto.

I have no illusions about how difficult it will be to win congressional support for this proposal. It will require a painful balancing of priorities, forcing the Congress to say no to some projects they may desire very much. It will mean that any tax cut must be accompanied by corresponding spending restraint. But I think the logic of the proposal will finally win approval for it or something very much like it.

The Congress in early 1979 did enact something like a balanced-budget amendment to the debt limit bill. Because of the deadline for passing that bill, the House had to grit its teeth and allow the amendment; also because of the deadline, the President had no alternative but to sign it.

The new law will require the President and the Congress to consider two alternative budgets each year. One would be in balance and the other would not. Presumably roll calls will be demanded on the two budgets and the public will then know whether their elected representatives voted for balancing the budget or not. The pressure to choose the balanced budget will be very great, especially in election years.

But the difficulty with the amendment is that Congress may well be voting to balance the budget during recession or sluggish growth periods, which would drive the country into deeper economic trouble. A few years of experience with this new law, and the logic of my proposal may prevail. My bill would ask for a balanced budget only when the economy can sustain it, and under those circumstances it permits no discretion, no other option. The budget *must* be in balance. On the other hand, in periods of recession, when stimulation of the economy is needed, the budget would be out of balance. The merit of the proposal is that the size of the deficit would be in direct proportion to need —slight in periods of low, modest growth, but much more substantial in response to weakening national productivity.

My bill would do part of the job of holding down spending, but not all of it. Milton Friedman, the Nobel Prize–winning economist, spotted this incompleteness immediately. He said his interest was not in balancing the budget but in holding down spending. He argued that a balanced budget would not necessarily reduce spending for two reasons. First, an increase in taxes could bring in enough revenue to balance the budget and still permit the government to go on its merry inflationary way of extravagant spending. Second, even without increasing taxes, a high rate of inflation would bring in an abundance of additional revenues as taxpayers' increased cash income moved them into higher and higher income tax brackets.

These are excellent points, but Dr. Friedman is only partly right. The balanced-budget requirement would, at the very least, inhibit spending. And anyone who has been in the Congress as long as I have knows how painful it is to increase taxes. They are much more likely to be cut. Any congressman who increases taxes must pay a political forfeit, but receives a nice, fat reward for reducing them. So though Friedman may be right on the economics of the situation, he is not right on the political factor. It's true that a legally enforced balanced budget would not hold down spending. He's certainly right there. More is required. But he should be grateful for small blessings. We are halfway home if we can get the budget balanced. Friedman won a Nobel Prize. He didn't win an election.

He wants spending held down and he wants it keyed to inflation. The higher the rate of inflation, the lower the level of permissible government spending. My amendment does more to achieve that than Dr. Friedman gives it credit for. It would require a surplus in the budget when the *real* rate of growth exceeds 3 percent, after allowing for inflation. But if the country is suffering from a rising rate of inflation which becomes higher than it has been estimated, the budget would then produce a larger surplus to match the rate of inflation. In fact, if that rate exceeds the estimate, the budget will be in surplus, even if the real growth rate is less than 3 percent. So the worse the inflation, the more severely my budget reduces spending.

Friedman's fear is that the Administration might deliberately estimate a very high inflation. Then, if the actual rate came in below the estimate, the budget could be in deficit above the 3 percent real rate of growth. But it's hardly likely that any administration would exaggerate inflation. Quite the opposite. In the years I have served on the Joint Congressional Economic Committee and have asked chairmen of the Council of Economic Advisers and Treasury secretaries to estimate inflation, I have found that the Administration consistently underestimates it. One year they estimated 2 percent and the actual rate turned out to be 10 percent for that coming year. Naturally, they don't want to be in the position of predicting that inflation under their economic leadership is going to get worse. What's more, such an official estimate could become a self-fulfilling prophecy, with labor and business alike making wage and price decisions that could only be more inflationary.

Whether Dr. Friedman supports my bill or not, I will enthusiastically support his. He's right that a balanced budget doesn't win the ball game; it might take you to first or second base. We need something else. Dr. Friedman has proposed a bill limiting spending, with the limitations becoming more exacting if inflation accelerates.

The Congress has been moving gently and slowly in that direction. Early in 1979 I was able to persuade the Senate to adopt my amendment to establish a goal for reducing spending to correspond to the Humphrey-Hawkins bill's goal to reduce unemployment and inflation. All three pieces of legislation have a similar limitation: they are goals, and only that.

My amendment would require the federal government to aim at a reduction of its spending as a percentage of the Gross National Product from the more than 22 percent in 1978 to less than 20 percent in 1983. This is a modest aim, in accordance with the announced objective of President Carter.

But it has a twofold weakness: first, it can be modified by the President if he decides that its achievements would not be in the national interest. Second, like the anti-inflation goal, it is subordinated to the unemployment goal. But it is useful because it sets, for the first time, the reduction of federal spending as an objective of national policy. And, to change it, the President would have to go before the nation and publicly admit that he was unable to hold down federal spending—something he would be reluctant to do.

My amendment was only a start. Senator Sam Nunn and others have persuaded the Senate, but not the House, to adopt an amendment to cut federal spending by 1983 to 19 percent or less of the Gross National Product (GNP). He provides a much stronger sanction for his spending limitation. He specifies that the Congress cannot put through a tax reduction unless there has been a steady reduction in spending as a percentage of the GNP that has proceeded on target toward 19 percent or less by 1983. In view of the strong propensity of Congress to cut taxes, especially in election years, the Nunn proposal is an ingenious and powerful discipline to hold down spending. At this writing it appears to have an excellent chance of being passed by both House and Senate. If it is not signed by the President, it may be passed over his veto. In view of the anti-spending sentiment in this country, I wouldn't like to be responsible for writing the President's veto message on that one.

Some may argue that my proposal to balance the budget, even buttressed with a mandated spending restraint, is a "pantywaist" approach when you need a tough, steel fist. Reliable polls indicate overwhelming support in more than thirty states for a constitutional amendment to balance the budget, even though states and cities would be among the first to lose their mammoth grants. I have already voiced, in another chapter, my objections to a constitutional convention, which are shared by many. But the balanced-budget amendment has weathered all objections—though it was slowed down—and the fact that the constitutional amendment proposal persists is testament to the depth and intensity of public feeling on the subject.

I oppose the constitutional amendment because it would turn out to be a serious economic blunder in the case of a recession, and could drive us into policies that would bring on tragic depression.

The argument that Congress could suspend a constitutional amendment under such circumstances does not hold water. Remember that the Great Depression lasted for ten consecutive years. How long could Congress keep voting to suspend such a deeply imbedded law? If anything could have caused a revolution in the country during the Great Depression, obedience to a budget-balancing clause in the Constitution would have done it.

What I am proposing is a law, not an amendment. It would mandate the sort of moderate and logical economic policies we should follow. During periods of average growth, the budget would be in balance; as the economy warmed up, the surplus would be moderate; with a move into high gear and exuberant growth of an inflationary character, a large surplus would be demanded to keep down federal spending. In the event of recession or depression, a large deficit caused by increased federal spending would stimulate the economy and push it back toward expansion again.

Perhaps the 3 percent real growth standard is too ambitious, leaving a margin for inflation caused by a slowed-down technology. In that event, a simple change in law (and no tampering with the Constitution) would adjust it. It could be moved in either direction, perhaps upward to 3.5 to 4 percent if the nation were enjoying a technology and capital investment boom. I have proposed 3 percent because that is the historical rate of economic growth for our economy. At that rate, the budget would have been balanced over the business cycle.

Above all, the Proxmire balanced-budget proposal would put a strong deterrent in the way of excessive spending: a clear-cut limit written into the law of the land. Any increases would have to confront the will of the taxpayers to pay for them. No longer would the easy availability of deficit financing destroy any attempt at discipline or restraint.

True, my bill should be backed up by a law like the Nunn proposal, specifically limiting spending and prohibiting tax reduction until the percentage of the GNP factor has been complied with. That's far more desirable than the limited restraint I've been able to get into the law. Together these two bills could go a long way to assure the country's emergence from the nightmare of inflation and year-after-year mammoth national deficits.

PART II: WHAT CAN YOU DO?

BECAUSE OF the recent excesses of the big spenders, and even more because of spiraling inflation, the country now seems in the mood to do something to slow the increase in federal spending. The previous section suggested what could be done; this section proposes how to get organized to do it. Fundamentally this means that the forces opposing big government spending have to be put on a basis that make them competitive with those who are pushing to spend.

This is a very big assignment because, with a few rare exceptions, whenever any organized group takes sides on a financial issue, it enters the lists on the side of spending.

Take businessmen, for instance. They are considered to be, and indeed are, more conservative than the rest of the country and theoretically more opposed to federal spending because it means more taxes and more regulations. Yet when they pressure their elected representatives at all, they are invariably in favor of spending. Like the rest of us, they identify with their own interests, not with other consumers and taxpayers. They identify with other producers. They are typically represented by a trade association. A businessman pays to support his trade association, and its job is to further his interests as a builder or contractor or *seller* to the government, almost never as a taxpayer. His own possible opposition to spending is silent and invisible. His support of spending, through his trade association's lobbyists, is direct and explicit.

Thus, though all of us in the Senate hear that, in general, American business wants less government spending and a balanced budget, we are constantly written to, phoned, called on, and buttonholed to spend here and spend there. Economy and the woes-of-inflation talk is just for the coffee shop and the bar. The spending talk is serious, and businessmen judge their elected officials on what they spend—for their particular business advantage.

The farmers are the same. They know that inflation, high interest rates, and high taxes are torpedoing their profits and that government spending has a lot to do with it. But when they ride in to Washington on their tractors, and storm congressional offices, they are not asking that the government spend less but that it spend more—more on farm support.

Though the workingman is always represented by his leaders as demanding more federal money for defense contracts, public works, and higher state, city, and federal salaries, this is often not his true position. I can tell you, from standing outside plant gates all over Wisconsin during the last thirty years, shaking hands with hundreds of thousands of typical American workers, that they are as much or more concerned with federal spending and its consequences than any other Americans. But no one organizes them in that direction.

As I have said, the spenders get what they want because they are so organized. They have no real opposition. The only surprise is that they don't get much more than they do.

In recent years, however, a few uncertain, sometimes crude and fumbling voices are being raised to hold down spending. One example is Proposition 13.

When Messrs. Jarvis and Gann put out their proposition to force California to roll back its property taxes on the ballot, most observers didn't give it a chance. To be sure, it was attractive to millions of California's overtaxed property owners. But, as I have noted, there was impressive opposition, including that of Governor Jerry Brown, who was emphatically and consistently against it, and major corporations that spent a lot of money fighting it, in spite of the fact that it was so ineptly drafted that the corporations were among the principal—if unintended— beneficiaries. State and local labor leaders crusaded against Proposition 13, and, in general, the media opposed it. A more moderate tax reduction program was put on the ballot to siphon off votes.

In spite of all this, Proposition 13 won by an incredible two-to-one margin.

Governor Brown set a new speed record for switching positions and became such a vehement partisan of the proposition that one poll showed a majority of Californians were convinced he had favored it all along. The message reverberated throughout the country. The congressional campaign of 1978 turned into a referendum in state after state to determine who could be the most enthusiastic crusader against big spending. A long established and ostensibly invulnerable star of the Senate, Charles Percy, faced a possible upset by Alex Seith, a Chicago lawyer who made government spending a big issue. In 1972 Percy had enjoyed the largest plurality in the country. In 1978 he had a much closer election. After the election he announced he was going to sit down and have a long person-to-person talk with the author of Proposition 13.

Another example is the resurgence in 1978 of the National Taxpayers' Union, the only organization that has put on an anti-spending crusade on a national basis.

It is lightly funded. It has a tiny handful of Washington staff people, including a bright, hard-driving, earnest young leader named Jim Davidson. It is the one and only anti-spending lobby —a tiny David taking on a whole series of Goliaths. It has been vastly outmanned and outdone financially by the pro-spending forces. But in 1978 it gathered speed and clout.

The National Taxpayers' Union (NTU) is the only group in

Washington that publicizes an annual, truly comprehensive spending scorecard tallying the votes of members of the House and Senate. They measure the performance of a congressman or senator on one criterion only: his voting record against spending. (Other conservative organizations will call a congressman's vote for spending a "wrong" vote if it relates to some social program, but a vote for spending in a military cause is considered "right.")

On the NTU scoreboard, *any* vote for spending—domestic, foreign, or military—is considered a wrong vote. The simplicity of their position has given them a quick and surprising influence far out of proportion to their size.

Their roll call is the only one that seems to get a rise out of senators in the cloakrooms. The day after it hits the press, senators will ask me, "Prox, how come you did so well and I did so badly?" Or, "This is going to kill me at home. It's just what that lying, distorting opponent of mine has been waiting for so he can stick me with the 'big spender' label."

Senators have good reason to worry about it. In the fall of 1978, I worked in a number of states to support various Senate and House candidates. Although there must be twenty or thirty records of congressmen's votes put out by various business, labor, consumer, environmental, education, and other groups, the only one that seems to make a big difference is the Taxpayers' Union scoreboard, in part because it is the only one that grades senators on *all* spending votes and the only one that considers every vote for spending a wrong vote.

In the Montana Senate race between Baucus and Williams, both candidates made the National Taxpayers' Union roll call the centerpiece of their campaigns. I flew out to help Baucus, who had one of the best economy records in the House. Though Williams claimed that Baucus's record wasn't good enough and declared he had NTU endorsement, Baucus won. The scoreboard publicized by the NTU was certainly an important factor in saving him.

The same thing happened when I went into Indiana, Illinois,

and Oregon to support other candidates. The spending issue was a big one, and the NTU was right at the heart of many contests. In a campaign year in which congressional spending broke all records, and with Senate races averaging $900,000 for each major candidate, this tiny, underfinanced group played a major part.

The answer is that the anti-spending sentiment in this country is so strong, yet so poorly organized, that when this small, unique band of opponents to government excesses came along, they were able to find support among the people against the pros, and win.

Merely consider what they have been able to do in pushing the proposal to call a constitutional convention to mandate a balanced budget. They began on March 1, 1975, and since then have persuaded thirty states to pass such a call against the interests of those states that have become addicted to billions of dollars of federal aid every year. When they started, it sounded like a sophomoric dream.

I have already indicated that I disagree with the whole concept of tinkering with the Constitution. But I am still amazed by the skill and tenacity with which the NTU has helped maneuver this amendment through thirty state legislatures against the vigorous opposition of the President, the leaders of both parties in Congress, organized labor (vehement against it), and the general reluctance of organized business.

There must be strong national sentiment behind them; they have been swept along by an obviously turning tide. I see them as a little platoon, perched on a raft, zooming downstream with the force of a current that has changed direction, a torrent of reaction to overspending, high taxes, and inflation.

What can we do to provide the kind of control and common sense this anti-spending force needs to score consistent victories?

First, we must get letters, calls, and delegations to Washington to oppose *specific* spending programs, organized by groups that represent large constituencies in this country. Such a thing, believe it or not, has almost never been done. I once asked Tom

Scott, a retired former staff director of the Senate Appropriations Committee, what was the proportion of witnesses who came before the Committee to support a spending program as compared with those who came to speak against it. His answer: one thousand to one.

As a senator, I receive more than a thousand letters every day. A few oppose spending in general. The supersonic transport fight is one of the rare occasions I can recall in twenty-two years for which I received any letters opposing a specific spending program. None of the visitors who call on me in my office ask me to reduce the funds to be spent on *anything,* yet when I meet the thousands on my trips back to Wisconsin, many, many will complain about federal spending. Again, almost never will a constituent say stop wasting money on a specific highway program or health or education or welfare program or on military weaponry or on housing the moon rocks.

What a contribution it would be to a better federal housing program if the expert economists in the Chamber of Commerce, for instance, should come before the Appropriations Committee and oppose specific billion-dollar throwaways they are convinced will not promote the housing of the poor. Let members of the AFL-CIO urge their experts to testify against waste in a particular public works program that is costing far more than it can ever deliver. Or let the National Education Association challenge the money the government is spending on a farm program.

Every one of these programs would be improved by challenge and debate—a genuine national debate with competing forces weighted equally on both sides.

Why doesn't this happen? Maybe in small part because every interest group is fearful that if it stirs up trouble against another group, there will be retaliation and it will lose some of its own Christmas presents. But, principally, it's just plain inertia.

Is it unrealistic to call for some kind of vigorous, large-scale interest group protest against waste? No. An interest group has a direct, materialistic concern in holding down the squandering of its members' tax money. It can say so and it will say so, if enough members ask for it. And it doesn't take very many.

The Chamber of Commerce or the National Association of Manufacturers would be good places to start, because their memberships are willing and eager to oppose spending if there is an opportunity to do so. Almost any major chapter of the Chamber of Commerce could pressure the national organization to consider taking such an initiative, let's say against public works as a starter. Put up to a referendum of members and presented in the right way, it would pass overwhelmingly.

Why don't the labor unions ever make a concerted drive against specific waste of federal money? Why don't Pennsylvania workers, for instance, protest to their senators and congressmen against the federal money about to be spent to fund a big dam in Wyoming that they can see, after realistic analysis, will cost far more than it's worth.

What happens now is that the Wyoming senator will go to the Pennsylvania senator and say, "Fred, I've got this dam in my state. It means a lot to the state; it can help me in the next election." Fred's friendly and he likes the Wyoming senator. He also wants to work him over a little later for a multibillion job program that would help Philadelphia. So he replies, "Look, you've been a good friend of mine. I want you back here. I don't think your project is worth the powder to blow it to hell. I can't support it, but I'll duck the vote."

This cavalier attitude is not a reflection of lack of integrity; it's a normal, human, predictable impulse to help out a friend when there's no countervailing pressure to do anything else.

Let's change the scenario a little. Suppose the union leader from Philadelphia, who had supported Fred, has talked to Fred and urged him to fight in the Appropriations Committee against the Wyoming dam, and suppose his visit had been buttressed by letters and phone calls from Pennsylvania constituents saying, "Don't spend our money on this turkey."

Fred's answer to his colleague from Wyoming then might go

something like this. "Look, I wish I could help you on this one. But my people just won't stand for it. I have letters, phone calls, and one of my strongest supporters has singled out your dam. And he knows what he is talking about; he has facts and figures. Sorry, old buddy."

That's the sort of thing that happened when the conservation groups turned the Senate around in less than a year on the supersonic transport. On that specific spending proposal there was specific, clear-cut, visible, audible opposition.

How can you, as an interested citizen, play a part in reducing the fatty waste in our government spending? I can only refer to that same favorite slogan: "Get Informed. Get organized. And get tough." One person can accomplish wonders with a little brass and a lot of persistence.

You can do it through any sort of organization you belong to: Chamber of Commerce, labor union, farm organization, political party, trade association, retired citizens, school group, or church group. Before you attend a meeting, prepare in advance. Pick out your most hated area of waste in the federal government and take some specific program in that spending area. Do some reading on it. Magazines and newspapers are full of such information. (The *Reader's Digest,* by the way, runs an article critical of a specific spending program almost every month.)

At the meeting try to steer the conversation around to federal spending. You'll hear lots of criticism but most of it will be general. You then come on with your pet example of waste. If you get general support, suggest a resolution putting your organization on record in opposition to the project. If the resolution is passed, suggest it be forwarded to your two senators and your congressman. Then ask your friends to sit down and write notes to one or all three. You will be surprised to find out how surprisingly effective even such a small campaign can be.

The interesting part of it is that for most senators and congressmen it will be one of the very few times in their experience that they ever receive letters of that kind.

A little stress in your letter about voting against spending and not just talking about it might help. No one likes his sincerity questioned.

Another way you can get tough has to do with campaign contributions. Many contributions go through the Political Action Committee of your company or labor union or other group. You can put a tag on yours indicating that your donation is based on the conviction that the candidate is going to vote no on a project that happens to be your pet peeve. An individual contribution, personally sent, can have an equal if not more direct effect. I have run for office nine times. In every campaign except that of 1976 I accepted campaign contributions, thousands of them, and I cannot recall *one* in which the donor in any way even hinted that the contribution was based on my opposition to a particular spending program or project (and I have opposed many). On the contrary, many were tacit or explicit thanks for supporting certain programs in the past and others urged me or my fund raiser to be sure to support certain federal outlays that were coming up.

Could we overdo opposition to spending? Is there a danger that, with the violence of national sentiment as expressed in Proposition 13 and the call for a constitutional convention, we might go too far and choke off the constructive role that only the government can play in warding off depressions and mobilizing our national resources?

The answer is certainly negative. The spending habit is going to continue for years to come, with the forces promoting it in the ascendance. And if and when inflation abates, the virulent spending fever will flare up stronger than ever.

What we need is to instill an opposition technique that will become habitual and sufficiently challenging to make each spending decision by the Congress truly competitive.

This book is an attempt to initiate that process.

(14)

Getting the Budget's Worth

LET US ASSUME that we have achieved a type of balanced budget, moving up and down between deficit and surplus, depending on the GNP. And we're much closer to that than you might think. Even more optimistically, imagine we have an organized national force doing battle to keep the lid on federal spending. There still remains a big job ahead, a big task that is being miserably handled right now: that is, getting the most for the taxpayers' dollar, getting your money's worth.

*

The President's budget is the big, decisive document from which all decisions flow. If the President, in his annual budget, calls for a 10 percent increase or for a balanced budget, the Congress has to go along or be in serious political trouble.

All financial activity in Congress begins with that presidential document. It commands respect not only because it comes from our one nationally elected official but because it is the product of thousands of man-hours of work in each of the agencies, of hard decisions and compromises, followed by a detailed challenge from the Office of Management and Budget (OMB), the director of which is the President's principal no man. After the OMB experts spend weeks of scrutiny of every detail, there is often a surprisingly detailed review by the President himself.

And this is how it should be. Nothing comes close to the

budget in establishing the nation's priorities and in determining how effective the President will be. It's the budget that underlies our military strength, help for cities, farm price support, highways, waterways, and space exploration. It greatly affects the force and direction of our foreign policy. The elderly, battered or abandoned children, college educations, medical care from year to year all depend on the budget. It also takes one dollar out of every four or five that you earn. In recent years it has been a major force in driving up the cost of living.

Truman, Ford, and Carter especially, but many other Presidents too, have devoted long weeks to the budget with the help of many distinguished experts, who often have made careers out of improving the process. Lately Presidents have suggested constructive innovations.

Yet, in spite of all these well-meaning, strenuous efforts, progress in bringing the unwieldy animal under control has been pitifully slow—far slower than the eternal rise of the deficit. Much, much more could and should be done.

*

Abolish programs and entire agencies? President Carter proposed that instead of an operation simply examining proposed increases in the budget, every agency should be required to start at zero and justify its expenditures from the ground up. This is an excellent principle. In practice it has made little headway. Almost every agency has friends in the Congress and the Administration who will fight any such drastic action. But the idea is so logical and appealing that Congress itself adopted the idea in "sunset" legislation, which would terminate every agency after a few years and require that it be re-authorized.

This should be easier in Congress than in the White House because we already have regular annual or biennial authorization bills and annual appropriations, so that we could easily require that each agency be re-created each year with no commitment to the future. But so far it has represented little threat to the established agencies, because the "keep-us-alive" constituency has worked even more potently on Congress than on the Administration.

Why has it been impossible to kill antiquated, obsolete, or otherwise worthless agencies? The answer is that it just isn't done, and probably won't be until the ax falls once or twice and it can be seen that it works. I would suggest that the President abolish at least one major department or agency *every year,* and one minor department *every month.*

I will even suggest two leading candidates for abolition. The Small Business Administration (SBA) does some good work that should go on. It is responsible, for instance, for providing disaster assistance to small businesses suffering from flood or tornado damage. This function could certainly be transferred to the Federal Emergency Management Agency.

The principal function of the SBA, however, which is to lend money to small businesses, is a wasteful program in almost every aspect. Only a fraction of 1 percent of the nation's small businesses get any assistance from the SBA, and it's based far more on political preferment than objective need.

The loans are provided at subsidized rates. With more than 16,000 banks in this country, virtually any sound business can get a market loan if it merits one. Of course, with a buddy in the Senate or the House, especially one serving on the right committee, a small businessman or his lawyer can often badger the SBA into providing a low-interest loan even when a high-interest loan at a bank is available. Technically that's forbidden by law. But it's not hard for the small businessman to get his friendly banker to say no to the loan. Armed with this turndown, the businessman works on the SBA through his congressman and, presto, receives a nice, fat, low-interest loan. Very unfair to the businessman's competition—but, after all, what are political contacts for?

The SBA also has been conned into giving risky loans that no banker would or should provide. In this case, the government not only loses money on subsidizing a low-interest rate but also loses the principal value of the loan. The SBA should be abolished.

*

Abolish revenue sharing? Here's a more than $6 billion annual program. The man who championed it and got it through is Walter Heller—a most unusual economist. He's a top-flight technical expert; he is also eloquent and convincing. Like most economists he is wrong as often as he is right. But he has such a rare and happy gift of selling whatever idea possesses him that, as chairman of the Council of Economic Advisers, he charmed and cajoled both President Kennedy and the Congress. He dominated fiscal policy well into the Johnson Administration.

But it was President Nixon who put into action Walter's most expensive aberration. In the sixties, Heller argued before our Joint Economic Committee that the federal government was such a remarkable producer of revenue that we had to find a way to get rid of its flood of income, or federal surpluses would stunt economic growth, drive up unemployment, and bring on ever-deeper recessions.

His answer was to give the states and localities regular grants each year with no strings attached. President Nixon bought it— he liked the idea of dispensing funds to states without the "massive red tape" of detailed guidelines and accountability. Naturally governors and mayors love it—it has to be their favorite program.

Billions of dollars, and *no* accountability. As I have said, the League of Women Voters made a two-year study of this program. And they found many who just did not know where the money had gone. Not only the governors, state legislators, mayors, and city council members, but even the press couldn't take an educated guess at where it had vanished.

One critic of the program said: "It's like payoff money to the underworld. You don't know. You don't ask. You put it on the stump and run."

After I began to speak out against revenue sharing in 1975 and 1976, I was given the glassy-eye treatment by city and county officials in Wisconsin. This particular federal handout was a precious boon. Nobody had to explain to the taxpayers what they did with it. If some strikingly self-serving or stupid expenditure had to be explained, they could always fall back on, "This didn't cost you a nickel. It came out of revenue sharing."

In a moment of wonderful frankness, one county official said to me, "Prox, get off that anti-revenue-sharing kick. This is the one way we can give ourselves a pay increase without getting massacred by the voters."

Maybe the mayor wants a limousine or a shiny, new fire truck or a public tennis court or golf course near his house. Revenue sharing is the answer.

So today we have the ridiculous dilemma of a deficit-ridden national budget, with revenue sharing agents handing out billions of dollars a year to cities and states, most of which have been running handsome surpluses themselves, balancing their budgets year in and year out, and currently reducing their taxes.

We are creating new agencies all the time, such as the Education Department and the Energy Department. The time has come to abolish revenue sharing and the Small Business Administration just as a start. They are obsolete and wasteful. Unless we can bring ourselves to stop programs as we start others, the bureaucratic underbrush and the fiscal overgrowth will smother us.

*

Abolish an agency a month? I am talking about a minor agency and here is a good candidate. It has the compelling name of the National Center for Health Services. Here is its record as provided by the General Accounting Office: "An examination of over $20 million of this agency's grants and demonstration contracts indicates that routinely they were not completed on time, cost up to five times the original contract, and contained low quality and highly questionable results."

I asked the GAO to examine how this agency managed its research and demonstration projects, which are the functions they are funded to perform. What I found was that the information bought and paid for with over $10 million out of the government budget, under one contract, was not only unavailable to the public but much of it was essentially unavailable to the National Center for Health Services itself.

This is a discouraging example of an uncompleted seven-year-old project, from which the government is having to pull teeth to get the data it asked for.

A one-year study originally costing $325,000 was to compare the costs of different medical arrangements, such as group practices, solo fees for services, use of paramedic personnel, and so forth. This ballooned into a four-year, $1.25-million project.

An evaluation in the third year, *after* the contract was extended to four years and by $930,000, found that "the work had generally been of such poor quality . . . of 48 papers [produced] only one had been published, and this in a journal of generally low technical quality," and that the work would neither "contribute to or expand the existing body of . . . knowledge . . . or be useful for policy formulation."

This sounds like á fleece. What they found, essentially, was that the people who were paid to study efficiency were inefficient. The project was finally cancelled—after a $1.49-million outlay—because of "poor productivity."

According to the General Accounting Office,

The Center lacks the ability to determine whether goals are being achieved.

Of 94 contracts awarded in 1974, 37 were sole source awards. The July 1974 report showed that 67% of all Center contracts active as of March 30, 1974, were noncompetitive awards.

Of the 22 contracts [reviewed by the GAO] 21 had from 2 to 17 modifications after award. Many of the modifications were for increases in time and contract amount and for changes in scope.

Here is an agency designed to improve health care delivery—
a vital and costly aspect of American life. The examination by
the GAO indicates that the center more than rivals the Pentagon
in cost overruns, modified contracts, and late deliveries.

*

Should agencies with similar services be forced to fight it out?
One innovation the Carter Administration has introduced that
could be very constructive indeed is a competition between agencies of the government that have very similar—even duplicate—
programs. The idea is that the Office of Management and Budget
will bring in experts from two agencies that are doing the same
thing and challenge them to justify their existence—in other
words, to describe any element of either program that is essentially distinctive from the other.

One person who witnessed such competition told me that it
was very bloody and intense. The battle quickly involved, of
course, the top agency honcho to ride to each agency's help when
the decision was to be made as to which agency would lose
funding and jobs. Supervising and carrying out this process takes
a tough-minded, no-nonsense approach and the kind of respected
authority that can only come from a President. The President
has to back the final decision to the hilt and be prepared to justify
it to the Congress and the public. These are battles that can be
won. But only the President can win them.

The attempt to make spending decisions systematically and on
a priority basis happened for the first time during the preparation
of the 1980 budget. A governmentwide ranking of decision packages for marginal programs was carried out. In all, 355 packages
were ranked, totaling about $35 billion and representing the
bottom 6 percent of programs initially recommended for funding
and the highest-ranking packages initially *not* recommended for
funding (2 percent).

The ranking process consisted essentially of three stages:

1. Each of the *four* OMB program associate directors (Na-

tional Security and International Affairs; Economics and Government; Human Resources, Veterans, and Labor; Natural Resources, Energy, and Science) ranked programs in his or her area by priority.

2. A consolidated "straw-man" ranking of all the packages reviewed by those program associate directors was assembled.

3. An all-day session chaired by the executive associate director for Budget was held to determine final rankings. With the straw-man ranking as a base, packages were reviewed and reranked in priority order. The result was that a number of programs were dropped and some, which previously had not been recommended, were added to the budget. In net terms, the whole process lowered total estimated outlays for 1980 by about $500 million.

An example of programs affected by the new rating system was School Assistance in Federally Affected Areas (Impact Aid). Based on the low priority of continuing Impact at the current level (relative to other programs competing for resources) it was decided as a result of the review to seek a reduced level of funding. The estimated saving was $140 million.

It should be noted that the basic intent of this government-wide ranking was not to reduce the size of the budget. Instead, the primary purpose was to assure that funding decisions were consistent, and that funding decisions ultimately made by the President would be based on a unified map of all the priorities.

*

The director of the Office of Management and Budget is inevitably a man who might be called the big panjandrum of spending control—the top kick, the head coach. He represents the kind of personal force the President can summon to throw into the fray. He needs the unreserved, full confidence of the President.

Bert Lance certainly had that, but when he was nominated, I spoke at length against the nomination on the floor of the Senate and was the only senator against it. I opposed Lance not because of any banking hanky-panky, of which we had no knowledge at the time. I opposed him simply because he had no qualifications for the job. Here was the most important appointment that President Carter would have to make with respect to his budget. Lance had no budget experience at the federal level nor at the state, city, or county level. And none in a private corporation.

Bluntly, he knew nothing about budgeting. And what chance had he had to develop knowledge about the complex federal government? Mr. Lance had not served a single day in our government in any capacity. Yet he was being told to take over the budget of the most complex government in the world. The only things in his favor were that he had the complete trust of the President and also had the right kind of personality—assertive, self-confident, persuasive. These were important traits that could have enabled him to win some tough budget battles if he had had the remotest idea of the nature of his job.

But he lacked the most essential attribute of all: a track record in the government that would have immediately commanded respect from the cabinet officers whose budgets he might have to cut, and from the Congress which would have had to be persuaded to go along with the President's economy moves.

Who would I have put in the job? Arthur Burns. Of course, in fairness to the President, Arthur Burns might have refused the job. It would have taken great coaxing to get him to take it because it would have been nothing but a headache for that remarkable man.

But Burns, or someone as much like him as possible, would have been ideal. I say this although I have frequently disagreed with Burns and opposed his reappointment as chairman of the Federal Reserve Board.

He is highly respected in and out of Congress, has been chairman of the Council of Economic Advisers as well as of the Federal Reserve, and is recognized as one of the leading economists in the world. He knows how to handle senators, congressmen, and cabinet officers and is able to win their cooperation. He is disliked by some people but always respected. He thoroughly understands the federal government and, above all, believes fervently in holding down spending. How vividly I recall his appearances before our Senate Banking Committee. I would be hammering away at the inflation problem and the Federal Reserve's responsibility for it. Burns would reply with a remarkably thoughtful and sensitive criticism of federal spending.

With Burns manning the Office of Management and Budget, I can see the President winning one anti-inflation battle after another—especially in the area of federal overspending. Burns would not only have the respect of Congress, but in any kind of an appeal to the country he could mobilize crucial business support in any area where the President was having trouble with his economy program.

*

Department Inspector Generals are a new phenomenon created by President Carter in 1978. The idea sounded exciting and had obvious potential: an officer in each big agency explicitly charged with finding and rooting out fraud. With the Attorney General estimating that fraud alone could be costing the government at least $25 billion every year, the new inspector generals might make a breakthrough in savings—but only in some departments where we are lucky enough to have a tough-minded, thick-skinned secretary who will back his inspector to the hilt and let the chips fall where they may.

It will take an unusual secretary to do that. After all, if the IG does his job well, the whole department, including the secretary, may turn out looking bad. Or take a department head. An eager and aggressive IG comes in and exposes chiseling right and left. What does that do to the head and his standing with his employees? How does it make the President look? Obviously these things can be done discreetly, quietly, without publicity. But it's not easy.

One change in the inspector general setup might give the new system a chance. Though outright fraud cases, of course, have to be reported directly to the Attorney General for investigation and possible prosecution, matters of waste—where most of the squandered money is involved—would simply be reported to the agency head for action.

In some, but not all, cases the agency head may use this information and eliminate the waste. It still won't be easy. If the new system doesn't show results in the next two years, Congress should consider changing the law, abolishing the present inspector general position, and authorizing a new type of IG who would be appointed by, and responsible only to, the Office of Management and Budget. An alternative would be to make these inspectors a part of the General Accounting Office, which is an arm of Congress, completely independent of the President. With the kind of impartiality and effectiveness the GAO has exhibited, an IG responsible to it alone would be able to work closely with the Congress to expose waste and fraud no matter how bad it made a cabinet officer or a President look.

*

The whistle blowers are the people who try to help control waste and fraud in their agency by calling public attention to it. They usually get knocked down for their pains. I have already discussed the experience of Ernie Fitzgerald in an earlier chapter. Unfortunately his experience is not rare, it's typical. Here are only a few brief examples.

John McGee worked for the navy in Thailand. He noticed that huge amounts of oil were being systematically stolen from the navy with the knowledge and help of some navy officials. He wrote me a letter of complaint about this. I called on the GAO to investigate. They confirmed McGee's story to a T and found that during one period more than half of all the fuel delivered in Thailand was being stolen. Was McGee rewarded? He was bullied, transferred against his will, denied promotions he could have expected as a matter of course, and suffered for years in the navy doghouse, in spite of my vigorous protests. To the navy's credit, McGee has been treated much more fairly in recent years. He has been allowed to suggest improvements in navy operations without penalty.

In April of 1978 Jack Anderson reported other examples.

David Stith, a black housing manager in North Carolina, revealed that millions of dollars of federal anti-poverty money were winding up in developers' pockets instead of helping the poor. His charges were confirmed by official investigations. But those responsible for the corruption continue in power. And the Department of Housing and Urban Development has subjected Stith to repeated punitive transfers and investigations.

Phil Vargas, son of Mexican migrant workers, who put himself through Harvard Law School, directed a study on "sunshine in government" for the Federal Paperwork Commission. It was a devastating indictment of government secrecy and manipulation of the Freedom of Information Act by federal bureaucrats. Unfortunately for Vargas, his superiors were themselves federal bureaucrats, and they ordered him to transform his study report into a whitewash. Vargas refused and was fired. He has been without regular employment since.

Aquilla Fitzgerald is a middle-aged black woman who challenged the Department of Transportation's hiring practices as racially discriminatory. The DOT, which, incidentally, has the worst minority hiring record in the federal government, got rid of her by a Russian-style technique. Her bosses forced her to take a psychiatric examination and booted her out on grounds of mental instability. Jack Anderson, however, learned that the psychiatrist who examined Aquilla Fitzgerald found her perfectly sane and recommended *against* firing her.

Richard Floyd, a National Security Agency employee, tried to bring to his superiors' attention certain gross mismanagement and contracting irregularities within the agency. He too got the psychiatric-test treatment, which was used as a weapon to fire him and quash an investigation of his charges.

Dr. J. Anthony Morris was a Food and Drug Administration microbiologist who was rash enough to protest the Ford regime's $120-million swine flu immunization program as not only unwarranted but dangerous. He was eventually proved right. Many who had the shots suffered serious effects, and some died. Damage suits against the government have reached into hundreds of million dollars. But Morris was fired by President Ford's minions.

These dismal stories cry out for some support for the whistle blowers. The President should single out for praise and promotion department heads who have had the courage and good sense to reward critics within their own bailiwicks.

This is an extraordinarily difficult action to pull off. The traditional "don't snitch" philosophy that has dominated so many of us since we were school children has to be faced—and in this case faced down.

*

The General Accounting Office, as I have often mentioned in this book, is a true and good watchdog over federal spending. It is headed by the Comptroller General, who is appointed for a single fifteen-year term. His independence is reinforced by a retirement program similar to that of a Supreme Court justice. He retires at full salary for life. He is exclusively responsible to Congress —and for housekeeping purposes he and his department are, in particular, responsible to the Government Operations Committees in the House and Senate and for funding to the legislative subcommittees of the House and Senate Appropriations Committees. But, in general, the GAO has 535 "bosses"—the members of the Congress. That makes the accountability so widespread that the GAO's independence is indisputably genuine.

The GAO has the expertise to command respect by means of four thousand professionals, located throughout the world: auditors, accountants, lawyers, investigators, and analysts of remarkably high quality.

In the numerous investigations they have made for me, I cannot recall a single instance where they have been proved wrong on the facts. Their reports are models of clarity and brevity.

The GAO saves your money in various ways. It has, for instance, helped the Office of Education collect some of the $287 million it had to pay to lending institutions because one out of every six college students (through September 1976) had defaulted on his or her tuition loan. The GAO recommended that bill collectors be hired and that the names of delinquent students be filed with credit bureaus. The latter had remarkably quick results.

As another example, the GAO disclosed the waste to the government caused by failure of officials traveling on federal money to follow the law requiring them to use the widely available discount airline fares. The GAO estimated that at least $470 million is spent unnecessarily in that fashion. They also found that federal agencies keep no records of discounts not taken and do not monitor travel expenditures to make sure the discounts are used.

The failure to use the GAO far more extensively than it does is a regrettable weakness of the Congress. Every committee that spends the public money should make sure that the agency it is funding is spending the money according to the law and that every allegation of fraud and waste is investigated. The GAO, as I have said, has been quietly but firmly pushing federal agencies to measure and to improve productivity. In this way it has already helped the taxpayer get his money's worth, and this with little encouragement and almost no recognition by the Congress.

A congressional committee that does not make constant and aggressive use of the GAO reminds one of a high school football coach with a 220-pound fullback who can run the hundred in less than ten flat and run over and through opponents all day but never gets in the game because the coach can't remember his name.

Creating agencies to save money may be a great idea. But we should start by using the ones we have.

*

The Congressional Budget Committees represent a noble, and so far ineffective, effort by the Congress to bring spending under control. The Budget Committees were at the heart of the Budget Reform Act passed in 1975 and hailed as a framework to make congressional spending more deliberate and accountable. It has not worked very well, perhaps because of a secondary objective of the bill, to wit, to prevent Presidents from slowing government spending by simply saying, "No, I won't spend it," to funding proposals passed by the Congress.

The law stopped the President from doing this, but permitted him to delay spending by sending a deferral—which the Congress had to vote to overrule—or by issuing a recision. In the case of the latter, he had to win support in both houses of the Congress for his decision not to spend the money. So both the deferral and recision segments of the law actually encouraged spending by making it so difficult for the President to say no.

The law does have one very strong anti-spending aspect, however, and that is the requirement that every member of the House and Senate must vote on a ceiling on spending. With the right sort of political consciousness around the country, this could be used as a powerful weapon to discipline the Congress to hold the line. For some mysterious reason, it hasn't worked. In 1978 I offered an amendment to balance the budget by cutting the ceiling down by $25 billion. Twenty-three senators supported my amendment. It lost. The vote could have been used throughout the country in the most spending-conscious election in years. But it wasn't.

If developed in the right way, a vote in both House and Senate on the spending ceiling could make a powerful national issue and be used advantageously in the next election.

But so far the Budget Reform Act has allowed the same dreary increases and huge deficits, after years of economic growth, that we suffered before the act was passed. This is so in spite of the fact that the membership and leadership in the Budget Committees have been very strong indeed.

Ed Muskie is without question one of the most forceful, intelligent, and respected members of the Senate. He has given the Budget Committee responsible and realistic leadership. He has fought unpopular, uphill battles to restrain spending both in his committee and on the floor, ably seconded by Senator Henry Bellmon, a thoughtful Republican senator esteemed as one of the best and brightest members of the committee by both Democrats and Republicans.

Budget Committee members certainly seem more consistent than most senators in *voting,* as well as talking, against increased spending. The staff works long and hard and does an excellent job of challenging the self-serving claims of other committees that tend to fight for all they can get for their constituencies.

The fact that Congress, with all this new institutional strength, hasn't brought down spending is a reflection of the coalition of power I have described in this book. It is also a reflection of the fact that the Budget Committees were simply superimposed on the established authorizing and appropriating committees. These previously enthroned groups retain not only their capacity to determine how the money within their jurisdictions is spent, but also the power, through their memberships, to exert heavy pressure on the Budget Committees when they are making their decisions, and when the final votes are taken on the floor.

*

American citizens have more strength than they realize. What finally counts is for them to reach the President of the United States on one hand, and 51 senators, 218 congressmen—a majority—on the other. In the preceding chapter, I suggested how to do this. With a President and a Congress truly committed, through political pressure from every sort of voter all over the country, the rest would follow.

The President would recommend the abolition of more agencies and subagencies than he would ask to create and Congress would go along. The President would appoint, as head of the Office of Management and Budget, a strong national figure, respected in the Congress and dedicated to a decrease in federal spending. Congress would honor and the President promote and not destroy all those who blow the whistle on fraud and waste. The Congress would use aggressively the new inspector generals and the General Accounting Office. The congressional Budget Committees would recommend balanced budgets, with flexible modifications to adjust to our economic swings.

After our experience in the past several decades, this may sound like never-never land. But it can happen if you as a citizen, voter, and taxpayer get into the act. If enough of us make it known to our elected officials with letters, phone calls, button-holing, and especially with our votes at the polls how we feel about their votes in Congress—not their general talk but their *votes* on each specific measure as it comes up—if we do this, we'll win.

The majority of the country is with us in sentiment—overwhelmingly, eagerly with us. But until now that sentiment has been unorganized, undirected, stumbling, and our massive budget and huge deficit show that it has been about as effective as a butterfly's hiccough.

What does it take? In this lazy, apathetic, indifferent political atmosphere of ours, it takes citizen action. That means you. Go to it.

INDEX

Index